NEVER ALONE

JUAN CANALES

NarratusCreative | NarratusPress

NEVER ALONE

©2017 Juan Canales. All rights reserved.

No part of this book may be reproduced or transmitted in any form, or by any means, electronic or mechanical, included photocopying, recording or by any information storage or retrieval system, without express written permission from Juan Canales.

ISBN: 978-0-9990752-0-3

Scriptures taken from the Holy Bible, New International Version®, NIV®. Copyright © 1973, 1978, 1984, 2011 by Biblica, Inc.™ Used by permission of Zondervan. All rights reserved worldwide. www.zondervan.com The "NIV" and "New International Version" are trademarks registered in the United States Patent and Trademark Office by Biblica, Inc.™

Scripture taken from the Amplified Bible, Copyright © 1954, 1958, 1962, 1964, 1965, 1987 by The Lockman Foundation. Used by permission.

Scripture quotations marked (TLB) are taken from The Living Bible copyright © 1971. Used by permission of Tyndale House Publishers, Inc., Carol Stream, Illinois 60188. All rights reserved.

Copyright © 2005 Integrity's Praise! Music (BMI) Sound Of The New Breed (BMI) (adm. at CapitolCMGPublishing.com) / My Other Publishing Company (BMI) All rights reserved. Used by permission.

Published by:

Juan Canales | neveralone-thebook.com
In partnership with:
NarratusCreative
P.O. Box 1413
Hamilton, OH 45012

Cover design: Daniel J. Marquez
Photo credits: Taylor Canales
Interior design: NarratusCreative | narratuscreative.com

Produced in the United States of America

In Loving Memory of Crystal Gayle Bledsoe
March 28, 1943 - June 9, 2015

Thank you for loving me and accepting me into your family. Thank you for trusting me with your daughter. We love and miss you every day!

DEDICATED TO...

...Anyone who has ever been told you were trash and would never be anything – that is a lie and great potential lies within you!

...Anyone who has been abandoned, rejected or abused – it is possible to be happy and for those places in your heart to heal!

...Anyone who wonders if there is more to life than what you've been through. Yes – and it's more than you ever dreamed!

THIS BOOK IS FOR YOU!

WHERE WE START DOESN'T DETERMINE WHERE WE FINISH!

CONTENTS

Acknowledgments *7*

Forewords *8*

Preface *10*

1. Starting Point 11

2. Life in L.A.: Abandoned 21

3. Life in L.A.: Father Figure 35

4. 2,066 Miles 45

5. Turning Point 53

6. My Brother's Keeper: Family of Five 65

7. My Brother's Keeper: Safe Keeping 73

8. Our Assignment 83

9. Dead Man Walking 97

10. The Fight of My Life: Denied 103

11. The Fight of My Life: Mistaken Identity 111

12. The Fight of My Life: A Man Without A Country 117

13. The Fight of My Life: Dual Citizenship 129

14. The Refinery 133

15. Purpose for the Pain 145

Afterword *155*

Photos *156*

ACKNOWLEDGMENTS

First, to my Heavenly Father who created me and has walked every second of this journey with me. Thank you for making a way!

To my wife, Liz, thank you for seeing potential in me and never giving up on me! I love you!

To my children – Nate, Mateo, Alex, Dominic and Marissa. My life has forever been changed by being your dad! You are my greatest accomplishment! I love you all!

To my Angel in heaven – One day I will hold you! I love you!

To Johana and Cristian – Look what God has done! Only He could do what has happened in our lives! I am proud of you and love you both!

To Yuli – I am so thankful you came into my life! I am grateful you are my sister and for our friendship!

To my mom – Thank you for giving me life! We have come a long way and I love you!

To Denise Chaney – Thank you for believing in me and helping me get my story out there! You are the best!

To my Pastors and Spiritual Parents, Russell and Beverly Hylton – From the day we met you have accepted me, loved me and invested in me! Thank you!

To our friends and family who have walked parts of this journey with me –Thank you for your love, support and prayers! I appreciate you all!

FOREWORDS

I first met Juan Canales in the Summer of 2012, when he and his family began attending our church, Bethel Family Worship Center, in Indianapolis, Indiana. After getting better acquainted, Juan shared his testimony with me and I knew instantly that he needed to write a book to share his story with the world. I'm so happy that he has put pen to paper so that the world will know how God can turn tragedy into triumph!

Juan is a survivor. He's an overcomer. Truly, he had something to "come over!" His journey from Honduras, to California and eventually to Indiana has the makings of an epic movie that wouldn't require Hollywood's A list actors to enhance it's storyline for the story speaks for itself.

Not only did he overcome the hardships of abandonment, homelessness and danger on the streets of Los Angeles as a young child, but he also overcame the emotions of rejection and unforgiveness.

Truly, God's hand of providence has guided Juan to a place of healing, restoration and wholeness. Today, he's using his testimony to help others who may be struggling with similar issues, to find hope and healing in the midst of adversity.

As you read this book, your heart will be drawn closer to the mission of Jesus, when He said, "For the Son of man is come to seek and to save that which was lost" (Luke 19:10). God knew where Juan was even when Juan didn't know where God was. The hand of God kept him, protected him and healed him so that you and I would be the recipients of his testimony of faith.

Russell Hylton, Lead Pastor
Bethel Family Worship Center
Indianapolis, Indiana

Juan Canales is a remarkable man. Despite having been through some of the most traumatic experiences anyone can have in this life, he has written a book that overflows with faith and hope. Your heart will break as you read how Juan's faith was tested in so many ways.

If you had to create situations that would result in me quitting and giving up, it would be what Juan actually lived through. And not only did he live through it, he's bringing life to many of us by using a difficult beginning to teach us how to walk closer with Jesus.

The way Juan handles such tragic subjects is raw and real. There is no sugar coating to his journey the Lord has taken him through. No one gets through this life unscathed. If you are hurting or struggling please read *Never Alone* because there is hope..... real hope! Juan Canales not only challenges me to seek out a deeper, more intimate relationship with Jesus, but through his faith, stirs in me a passion to lead a life filled with boldness and courage.

Throughout the book Juan shows how great God is. No matter what you are going through, He has a great plan for you. Everything is possible through God and only God!

When you leave this book, you will be a different person than when you came in.

Tyler Walker, Minister of Operations
Bethel Family Worship Center
Indianapolis, Indiana

PREFACE

This is a true story. It is my story. It is just one story out of millions out there yet to be told. To the best of my ability I have retold this story, knowing certain pieces may not quite be in the right order, but they did happen. This story is a tell all! If you give me a chance I will tell you all about my encounter with a love I had never experienced before! You will see how a collision with grace, forgiveness and mercy transformed my life and those around me! My story doesn't end as this book ends – it is yet unfolding. Praise God – it is still unfolding!

CHAPTER 1

STARTING POINT

"I was thrust into your arms at my birth. You have been my God from the moment I was born."
Psalm 22:10 (NLT)

NEVER ALONE

We all begin this life on Earth with a starting point. Each one is different. Factors like: who we are born to, where we are born, the culture of our family, religious beliefs and even traditions all play a part in our *Starting Point*. Actually, most of us experience many starting points in life: beginning an education, developing a relationship or working a new job, to name a few. Those are starting points we may have some control over, if not total control. The beginning of life though is completely different. We have no control over that!

We often hear stories of our ancestors, stories of our birth and early childhood, things we would never know unless someone passed that story on to us. But what do you do when you don't have a lot of stories to draw from and you have very few, if any, memories of most of your siblings and extended family? What do you do when large pieces of your life are missing and it doesn't make sense? Life seems like a puzzle and there are missing pieces. What do you do when the pieces that you do know seem too crazy to even be true?

For a long time I have known that I have a story to tell. I know that God has done way too much in my life to keep it to myself. However, there are parts of my life that just didn't make sense. The pieces just didn't fit. I have been on a journey trying to connect the dots, trying to find the missing pieces of my life's puzzle. I have retraced stories and time lines to make sense out of what I knew about my *Starting Point* all the way through my early teenage years. There are some things I don't remember simply because I was too young and some things that I blocked out. However, on this journey of piecing my life together and telling my story, memories have been triggered. Events that were tucked away in my mind have risen to the surface and have helped me make sense out of those memories I do have. I continue to be overwhelmed with God's love towards me. As I look at my life so far, there are countless times I could have been dead. It is evident that before I even took

STARTING POINT

my first breath I was *Never Alone*! I will always be grateful that He loved me before I loved Him!

It must have been a beautiful day in Choluteca, Honduras. My parents decided to go to a beach on the Gulf of Fonseca, which is part of the Pacific Ocean, with three of my older sisters for the day. My mom was seven-months pregnant with me. I'm sure my sisters, who were five-years-old, two-years-old and 10-months-old, were having a blast playing with our parents in the ocean. I imagine my mom laughing and holding on to the girls as they fall into the waves. I suppose they even swam out a little ways. My mom has said that a couple of times the strength of the waves literally knocked her down. In fact, they were having so much fun that they left the shore a little too late and missed the last bus, so they had to walk back.

My dad, mom and sisters began their walk home. Two hours into the journey, my mother started having contractions. She knew what was happening. At the age of 24, I would be her sixth child. She obviously knew she was having contractions and was concerned because she also knew it wasn't time for me to come yet. I wasn't due for almost three more months. My mom knew she had probably over done it that day. She had taken some pretty hard hits from the waves and a two-hour walk home after a full day at the beach hadn't been in the plan. Even though the contractions were mild they were enough to scare her into stopping at a hospital.

My mom describes the hospital as being dirty. There were holes in the ceiling and in the walls. The doctors were on strike for some reason and my mom was left in the care of the nurses. She said they began to push on her stomach. For an hour – maybe two – they were on top of her, pushing downward in an attempt to push me down the birth canal. The pain was excruciating for her, but it worked. Ready or not, there I was. Around 9 p.m. on January 22, 1984, almost three months early, I was born. They named me Juan Pablo after Pope John Paul. My mom was thankful that, especially for my being born so early, I seemed to be healthy. The only real issue I had

13

was staying warm enough. She said that they had to keep me under blankets otherwise I would shake uncontrollably. The hospital kept us for a couple of days before sending us home to my dad and sisters.

About a week after I was born my parents moved us to the other side of Honduras to Tela, Atlantida. Tela borders the Caribbean Sea in the Northern part of Honduras. Some of the stories I've heard about that time aren't too surprising. They have a reoccurring theme: my dad was gone a lot, leaving my mom home to care for her four youngest kids. Her two older children from her first marriage lived with their father.

My mom told me that during the first several months of my life, there were times she thought I was dying. I would cry, scream and shake a lot. She wasn't sure what was going on with me. Eventually, I quit doing that, but then I developed a horrible skin issue because of the sand and salt water. She had to boil my clothes before putting them on me. We lived in Tela about a year before my dad moved us to another part of Honduras.

> **AT THAT POINT IN MY SHORT LIFE, I GUESS YOU COULD SAY I HAD DEFEATED DEATH AT LEAST TWICE.**

At that point in my short life, I guess you could say I had defeated death at least twice. When my mother figured out that she was pregnant with me, my sister was only about a month old. One of my mom's friends kept trying to convince her to have an abortion. Thankfully, even though she knew it would be hard with so many children so close together, my mother chose to have me. The second death-defying act was surviving a preterm birth in a country with inadequate medical care over 33 years ago.

On this journey of piecing my life together I have had to rely on stories.

STARTING POINT

Stories from my mom, a few of my sisters and other relatives have helped me piece some things together and actually triggered more memories. These memories have taken me back to when I was a young boy in Honduras. Bear with me as I try to relay them here. It's safe to say that some of these memories aren't in the right order.

Honduras is a beautiful country. Mountains stretch over most of it and there are beaches on the northern and the southern borders. We left Honduras when I was about 5-years-old, but I do have some memories of being there. Some of the stories from those first five years of my life are sketchy. I don't have the complete story and since I have only seen one baby picture of myself, I have no visuals to help trigger more memories.

For most of my life I had basically two memories of my childhood in Honduras. The first is of a place we lived in. I call it my "Happy Place." It seems like this place was near the beach. I remember the shade of palm trees and coconuts. The ocean was calm. I even remember eating coconut bread. It was so good! Sounds great doesn't it? My "Happy Place" had only one room and the floors were sand – it was a structure that we would consider a hut.

I had always heard my dad say that when I was a child I had polio. According to him, the doctors said that I would never walk. I'm not sure if this is true, because being the con man that he was, he could have used this story as a way to make people feel sorry for him and give him money. But it seems like I do have memories of dragging myself around through the sand of that little hut-like room. I have some faint memory of not walking right and I do remember him massaging my legs. If the story he tells is true, then God performed a miracle by healing me!

The second memory is of being at home with my mom and dad. Some men came in and began to beat up my dad. I'm not sure what he had done, but I watched them keep pushing his face down into some water. I was terrified. Based on the fragments of memory that I can string together, I must have

NEVER ALONE

been somewhere between 2 and 4-years-old when this happened.

As I have been piecing my childhood together, I was told something that didn't surprise me, but actually left me with more questions. I have always known that I had sisters who were raised in an orphanage. At some point, when I was around three-years-old, my sisters had been left with a neighbor to look after them. I'm not sure for how long – another unanswered question. By this time my parents had another child after me, so three of my older sisters and my younger sister were put into an orphanage. That is where they grew up – in an orphanage in Santa Rosa de Copan, Honduras. I always wondered why I had not been abandoned at the orphanage. Last summer I found out that I actually had been! I was taken to the orphanage with my sisters.

Once again, I wasn't surprised by this news, but it does make you feel a little uncomfortable when you're 32-years-old and just learning something so significant from your childhood. Are there other significant events I know nothing about? Yet another one of my unanswered questions.

When I was told this information about the orphanage I had a flash of a memory. It was one of the only memories I have with my siblings in Honduras. In my mind I saw a quick flash of me lying on a bed or pallet with three or four of my sisters. That was it. It was over. Which leaves me with more questions. Was this in the orphanage or at home before we went to the orphanage?

One of my older sisters told me that I was around 3-years-old when we were taken to the orphanage. Initially, I was taken to the girl's orphanage with my sisters. Was this a memory I had from that orphanage? At some point I was taken to the boy's orphanage. It is unclear how long I was with my sisters before I was taken to the boy's orphanage. It is also unclear how long I was in the orphanage period. I have heard everything from a few weeks, to a few months, to a year. Who knows?!

STARTING POINT

A few weeks after learning about my being in an orphanage a new memory surfaced. Maybe this memory was one I had blocked, perhaps in an attempt to not remember the orphanage. In this memory I was sitting on the floor in a room. I was just looking down as a woman called my name.

"Juan," she kept saying. I didn't look up. I didn't recognize her voice. Finally the woman came over and picked me up. I looked at her. It was my mother. I asked my mom about this memory. She confirmed that it was in fact what happened when she came to pick me up from the orphanage. She went on to tell me that I wouldn't let her out of my sight after that. I still don't know how long I was in the orphanage or how I got out and my sisters didn't. How had all of this happened?

As a result of all of the conversations with my mom and my sisters, a couple of more memories of Honduras resurfaced. My sisters would occasionally get to leave the orphanage to visit my grandmother. Maybe I was still in the orphanage too – I don't remember. We would go to my grandmother's and she would give my sisters and me choco-bananas – which are chocolate covered bananas. I love choco-bananas! Now I know why. Another memory – another piece of my life – in place.

This next memory must have been after my mom got me out of the orphanage. Often my mom and I would stay up late at night waiting on my dad to get home. My dad would be gone anywhere from a day, a few days to maybe even weeks. While my mom and I would wait for him, we would talk and look at the sky. Around midnight there was an orange flower that bloomed. It was beautiful.

Sometimes my dad would take me with him on day trips and eventually I caught on to what he was doing. I remember going to a lady's house. My dad would tell her kids and I to stay outside. We were not allowed to go into the house, so for hours these kids and I would have to stay outside. They didn't like me. They wouldn't play with me. Maybe I didn't like them either since

NEVER ALONE

I somehow knew that my dad wasn't supposed to be there with their mom. Maybe they didn't like me because they had a bike and I would take it from them – that is how I taught myself how to ride a bike. I was quite proud of myself for that, but I hated going there. I understood at a very young age that my dad cheated on my mom. So, in those memories where my mom and I stayed up at night waiting on him, I knew he was up to no good.

I have another memory that has always stuck in the back of my mind. One that I cherish! As I have grown older the memories surrounding it faded so I had trouble remembering if it had actually happened in Honduras or somewhere else. I could see myself in the arms of a fair-skinned, white-haired woman. I'll never forget her eyes. They were blue. In my memory she was talking to me and I felt safe with her. She was kind and gentle. There was something different about her. Something I hadn't experienced before. The thought of her and that moment have stayed with me.

Growing up, this memory would cross my mind. I often wondered who was that fair-skinned, white-haired woman with blue eyes. How could I remember this single moment but not remember who she was? Was she from Honduras or somewhere else? As I got older and this memory would come to me, I began to recognize that what I remembered as her talking to me, was actually her praying for me. I guess when it actually happened I was too young to understand that she was praying for me or maybe I didn't know what prayer was until I was much older.

One day, I was describing this memory to one of my sisters who grew up in Honduras. I was not expecting her to know exactly who I was talking about. As I described this woman's skin, hair and eyes, she says, "That's Mama Rosa! She is our great grandmother!"

Wow! After all these years I finally knew this was a real memory from Honduras – a memory of my great grandmother holding me and praying for me. Sometimes I wonder, was it her prayers that spared my life from

STARTING POINT

everything that lie ahead of me?

The best I can piece together is that we left Honduras for the United States when I was around 5-years-old – my parents and I and my sister Johana, who is four years younger than me. I'm not sure that I realized what was going on. I definitely didn't realize that almost three decades would pass before I would see Honduras again. We left behind grandparents, aunts, uncles and cousins – even nine of my siblings. My mom and dad each had three kids from previous relationships and together they had five. Four of my sisters were left to grow up in an orphanage. My half siblings had other family members that raised them. About 28 years would go by before I would have the opportunity to go back to Honduras. I was able to meet a few more of my sisters, but I have yet to meet all of my siblings.

We left Honduras sometime in the beginning of 1989. I'm not sure how long it took us, six months maybe almost a year before we made it to the U.S. I only know that after going through Guatemala, we stayed in Mexico for a long time. My mom would make food to sell. I'm not sure what my dad did. As usual he was away a lot. In Mexico, I was being taught things that Mexican nationals would know about the country. I remember learning the Mexican National Anthem. That was my dad's insurance plan. If immigration agents picked us up when crossing the border into the U.S., we would need to convince them we were Mexican. If we were deported my dad wanted us to go back to Mexico so that we wouldn't have to start all over from Honduras.

In 1990 my dad, mom, sister and myself entered the United States through Douglas, AZ. We entered without inspection – undocumented. I guess we should just go ahead and say it – illegally. I was 6-years-old, my sister was around two. Most people come here for the American Dream. Don't get me wrong; I am thankful that I had the opportunity to come to the U.S. If I hadn't I wouldn't have my wife and children. However, my next several years would create more broken and missing pieces to my childhood. It would be far from the American Dream!

CHAPTER

2

LIFE IN L.A.

Part 1: Abandoned

"You number and record my wanderings; put my tears into your bottle - are they not in your book?"
Psalm 56:8 (AMPC)

NEVER ALONE

I sat in the back seat of the car that drove us over the border from Mexico into the U.S. I was a little surprised. In Mexico we had prepared for the possibility that we would be stopped and detained. We had gone over and over what to say and what not to say. There we were in Arizona and our car hadn't even been stopped. We just drove right over the Border. I'm not sure how far we drove that day; I just remember that the car drove us to a mission. That mission in Arizona was our first stop in the United States. I don't remember how many days we were there, but they fed us and gave us each a few articles of clothing. We left Honduras with very little. We left Mexico with even less. Before a week had passed, the mission had bought us Greyhound tickets. We were headed to Los Angeles.

It was daytime when we left Arizona and it was still daytime when we got to L.A. *So this was the great and wonderful place I had been told we were going to*, I thought, as I looked out the window. I don't know why, but in my head I had pictured nice neighborhoods – big houses with bigger yards and white picket fences around them. This was very different than I had imagined.

When we got off of the bus we walked for what seemed like forever. It definitely felt like forever with my little 6-year-old legs. We were headed to where a man, I'll call him Mr. K, lived. I'm not sure if my dad knew him personally or had only heard of him, but he had been told that Mr. K would help us out. Mr. K spoke Spanish, but I'm not sure if he was from Honduras. He had a wife or a girlfriend who lived with him who spoke Spanish too. Mr. K managed some apartments so after spending a few nights in their apartment he moved my family into an apartment near him. My parents had an arrangement with him. In order for us to live there, my dad would help out with maintenance, painting and cleaning around the property and my mom would help with cleaning apartments as they were vacated. We didn't have any furniture in our apartment, but we had a roof over our head.

I overheard conversations between Mr. K, his lady and my parents. They

LIFE IN L.A.: ABANDONED

all agreed that I needed to go to school. There was one problem though. I didn't speak English. Mr. K's lady began teaching me. I remember sitting at a round glass-top table with her. She taught me how to count to 100 in English. She also taught me what I would call American manners. She would tell me things that I shouldn't do at the dinner table. She also told me not to point with my middle finger. In some Hispanic cultures when you point, instead of using your index finger, you use your middle finger. I believe we lived in that apartment for about a year before we moved.

The next place we lived was off 52nd and Vermont in South Central. I was 7-years-old when I started my first school in the United States. I didn't go to kindergarten. I started school in the 1st grade in South Central L.A. speaking practically no English. It seemed as though I was the only Hispanic kid in the school. I felt alone – like I didn't belong there. I only remember one man that spoke Spanish. He worked in the school office. Neither my teachers nor my classmates spoke a word of Spanish. I didn't really have any friends. As a matter of fact, I would get made fun of and beat up by some of the older kids on a regular basis. They knew I didn't belong there and I quickly realized I didn't belong there either.

After school I would walk past the fence that walled the school in like a compound. I would walk down 51st street towards Vermont hoping no one would mess with me. I turned left at the corner onto Vermont to get to the apartment my parents rented above a little supermarket. We rarely went outside of our apartment. It wasn't safe. It didn't take us long to figure out that we were in a part of the city that was run by gangs. I remember staying inside our little apartment with hardwood floors, which is where we slept when we lived there because we still had no beds or any furniture – at all.

On the weekends my dad would ref soccer games for Hispanic leagues for money. Sometimes he would take me with him for the day. When I wasn't watching him ref I would play with the other kids there. One of those days after I had gone with him we took a bus back to our apartment. We had just

NEVER ALONE

gotten off the bus at the corner where we lived when two guys walked up to my dad and one of them pulled out a knife.

"Money," he said. Even though my English was broken I understood that we were being robbed.

My dad was saying, "It's okay man!" raising his hands above his head. I moved closer to my dad and I saw that the man had the knife right up to my dad's stomach.

Out of nowhere I heard the squeal of tires and there were police lights shining on us. One of the guys took off but the police got the man holding the knife before he could get away. It turns out that the police had been driving by when they saw my dad with his arms up. While holding the man at gunpoint, the officers asked if we were okay. My dad told them that he had just came from his job of reffing soccer – which was true. He was still in uniform and had his duffel bag. He then proceeded to tell them that the guy who ran off had stolen $1500 from him – which was not true.

The guy who had the knife was arrested. My dad was given a case number and instructed to show up for court. I remember going with my dad to the courthouse. He gave a statement that he had been robbed of $1500 and the court awarded it to him. What he didn't realize was the family of the man he falsely accused of robbing him, lived right around the corner from us. They weren't happy about the extra charges brought on by my dad's lie. I think the family ended up agreeing to pay the $1500 in exchange for a lesser charge. Needless to say we moved within a week after my dad got that money.

From South Central my parents moved us to an apartment off of 7th and Magnolia on the west side of L.A. With the money my dad scammed out of the robbers he was able to get us a car and buy some furniture for our apartment. It was the first time we had furniture of our own since we lived in Honduras. I'll never forget this place for two reasons.

First, the L.A. Riots started right after we moved in there. It was the end

LIFE IN L.A.: ABANDONED

of April 1992. I remember watching it on TV. You could see buildings and cars burning, windows being busted out, people running in and out of stores carrying things. The police walked the streets in a group formation. This went on day and night for several days. It was scary. My mom, sister and I didn't go out. My dad would leave for hours at a time though. I began to put things together after he came home with stuff I knew we didn't have the money for. All of a sudden we had new clothes, shoes, TV's, cameras. I even got a bike! More stuff than we could use. He brought things home more than once. As we watched the chaos in Los Angeles unfold on television, he himself had been out looting.

The second reason I will never forget this place is because this is where we lived when they left me. My dad knew some people from Honduras who were willing to pay him to bring their family member into the U.S. Just a few weeks after the L.A. riots ended, by the end of May 1992 my dad, mom and little sister Johana left me in Los Angeles to go back to Honduras.

"You're going to stay here with Julia. We'll be back soon," they told me. I was 8-years-old. With no warning and no explanation as to why I couldn't go with them, I was left with this lady they thought they could trust. Julia moved into our apartment with me. I don't even know how they knew her or why they thought they could trust her.

About a week or two later I was walking up the stairs to the apartment. I looked over towards the parking lot and noticed Mr. K driving my parent's car out of the gate. *That's weird*, I thought. When I opened the door to our apartment I was surprised to see almost all of the furniture that my dad had just bought – gone! The apartment was almost empty. As I'm trying to make sense out of what's going on, Julia says, "Juan, your parents have died. We can't stay here any longer. You need to get your stuff and find somewhere else to live."

I don't remember asking her any questions about what happened to them

NEVER ALONE

or what happened to all of our stuff. I simply went and grabbed two shirts. I remember one of them was red with a white stripe. I grabbed some other things, put them in my backpack and left. I walked out of the apartment, went over to the metal stairs and just sat there. I didn't know what to think. I didn't know if my parents were really dead. I had no family in L.A. and didn't know how to get a hold of my parents in Honduras. I was 8-years-old, abandoned and homeless in L.A.

One of the neighbor ladies must have seen me sitting there crying. She offered to let me stay the night in her apartment. I only stayed there for one night. I heard her and her husband arguing in Spanish. "He can't stay here. That's another mouth to feed!" her husband said. The next morning I left.

I probably didn't eat for a day or two. I just walked around the part of the neighborhood that I was familiar with between Korea Town and MacArthur Park. I found some cardboard in dumpsters and pulled out clean, dry pieces to sleep on. The cardboard also served as a sort of shelter – a good hiding place so that I wasn't easily visible. I found small alleyways to sleep in between buildings that were just big enough to walk through. I would steal candy, gum – anything that was small enough to fit in my pockets or down my pants. I would eat what I could and sell what I didn't eat for some change.

There was a particular parking lot that was nearby several stores. People would park their cars there for a quick run into these stores. I figured out that at certain times of the day a tow truck would come through the lot. I also learned that by watching that parking lot long enough and paying attention to who got out of what car, I could make a buck or two. I would remember who went in to which store. When I saw the tow truck start to hook up their car to be towed, I could run and tell the people and they would give me money so that they could keep their car from being towed.

I also began to notice that other homeless people would pull cans and plastic bottles out of the trash. They would carry around bags and bags of

LIFE IN L.A.: ABANDONED

them. It didn't take me long to catch on that they were getting money for other people's trash. I began doing that too. It helped me to be able to get some food in my belly. When I didn't have any money to buy food and I was tired of eating whatever I could steal from the convenience stores, I would look through dumpsters at some of the restaurants. Sometimes, what I found in the dumpsters tasted better than what I would have stolen at the convenience store.

I would use public bathrooms at fast food restaurants to wash my face and hands. When my shirt or pants would start looking too dirty I would change into my other one. I washed my dirty clothes out in the bathroom sink. At a young age I realized that I had to use what I had available and make it work.

> **SOMETIMES, WHAT I FOUND IN THE DUMPSTERS TASTED BETTER THAN WHAT I WOULD HAVE STOLEN AT THE CONVENIENCE STORE.**

I stayed mostly to myself. I was afraid to ask anyone for help. I had been taught to stay away from the police (probably because we came to the U.S. illegally) and since the people my parents had trusted to take care of me put me on the street, I trusted no one. Most days I would walk over to MacArthur Park. It was only about a 10 or 15 minute walk down 7th Street. I would look for cans or bottles to recycle. Sometimes I would wash my face and hands in the water fountain. Occasionally, some of the other homeless people would speak to me. Even though by now I spoke some broken English I was afraid to say anything. I just kept walking.

One night I was on my way back to the area where I was going to sleep for that night. I hadn't gotten too far away from MacArthur Park when all

NEVER ALONE

of a sudden someone grabbed me from behind and pulled me into a small alleyway. I tried to get away by kicking and screaming, but he picked me up and threw me face down on the ground in the alleyway. I was still kicking and screaming while he was on my back punching me and telling me to shut the f--- up. He kept pushing my face down into the concrete. When he wasn't punching me, he began to rape me. I could feel the little pieces of gravel and dirt piercing my cheeks. I was crying as those pieces dug in farther and farther. When he was done he got up and walked away.

I laid there crying for a few moments before I pulled myself up to see how badly my face was bleeding. I could taste blood in the corner of my mouth. Even after he hit and punched me the way he did, I managed to get myself up and go to a nearby bathroom. I was bleeding from my face and private area. I cleaned myself up and changed my clothes.

A lot changed after that night. I was way more cautious. I would change up my routines and the routes I walked. I was always afraid. I was constantly looking behind me. If I noticed a man walking behind me I would cross to the other side of the street. I didn't want anyone around me. I was angry! I was 8-years-old and knew enough to know that none of this should have been happening. Why wasn't anyone there for me? Why didn't anyone care?

Not too long after that horrible night I was able to work out an arrangement with the owner of the convenience store right in front of the apartments where my parents left me. "You work for me – you sleep there," he said in his broken English, pointing at a pile of boxes in a corner on the floor of the store. My parents had been gone for two, three, maybe four months by that point. It seemed like forever. This arrangement was no doubt the best thing that had happened to me since they had left. A place to sleep – inside – was what I had been hoping for.

I stocked whatever shelves the owner told me to. I took out the trash, swept and even unloaded a delivery truck. In return, he made sure I had

LIFE IN L.A.: ABANDONED

something to eat at least once a day and more importantly, that I had indoor shelter at night. I'd stack up the boxes on top of each other in a corner and pretend they were a bed. It was good! Then, one day after maybe three weeks or so, he told me I couldn't stay there any longer. I figured it was because he didn't need another mouth to feed. So, just like the day Julia told me I couldn't stay at our apartment any longer, I got my stuff and left. No questions asked. I just left.

It was evening. I started walking down 7th street, but this time I went in the opposite direction that I would normally go. For some reason I decided to leave the only area I really knew in L.A. It seemed like I walked for a long time. When I finally stopped, I sat on some steps across the street from a bar. I watched as the people went in and out. It was noisy. Maybe that's why I picked that place. I felt safer there at night. It was brightly lit with a lot of lights and you could hear music and people talking. Maybe I didn't feel as alone there or I thought if someone tried to grab me, I'd have a better chance of being heard.

After sitting at the same place for about three or four – maybe five nights – a lady noticed me. She had been going into the bar every night and on her way in she would say "Hi," to me. I would wave back to her. One night about an hour after our little exchange, people started leaving the bar in groups. They were almost running out. *What is going on*, I wondered. I hadn't seen this happen on the other nights I had been sitting there. Before I knew it, I was watching the lady who told me "Hi" being dragged out of the bar. A man was dragging her by her hair and punching her in the face. I froze. Memories of seeing my dad beat my mom came flooding back to me.

Eventually, the guy left, but she wasn't moving. She was just lying there. Nobody was even checking on her. I walked over to her. I moved her hair so I could see her face. It was bloody. She began to try to move around.

"I need to get home to my kids," she told me in Spanish. She said it again

NEVER ALONE

as she tried to lift herself off the ground, but she couldn't. I stood up so she could use me as a crutch. I remember she took her heels off and leaned on me for extra support. We walked a ways that night. Further away from where my parents left me on 7th and Magnolia.

"Why do I see you sitting there every night?" she asked me as we walked up to her apartment. I explained to her that I had been told that my parents were dead and the people my parents left me with had put me out on the street. "Come in," she said. "We'll figure things out in the morning." I was so relieved! A place to sleep – inside. Even if it was just for a night I was still relieved.

Maria let me sleep in the living room that night, but not on the couch. I slept on the floor and I didn't care! I was inside and there was carpet! The next morning Maria told me to go take a shower. It was probably the first time I had taken an actual shower since I had been put on the streets. It was great! Afterwards, Maria sat me down and asked me a bunch of questions. When it seemed she'd heard enough she told me she would let me stay with her and her kids. She had a girl who was about my age and a boy who was younger.

I had a question for Maria too. "Why do you go to that place every night?" I asked her in Spanish. She seemed like a nice lady. I believe she was from Venezuela. *She doesn't belong there,* I thought to myself.

"I work there," she replied. "I'm a fichera." A fichera is a lady who entertains men at a bar, keeps them company and gets them to buy more and more alcohol.

From time to time Maria's kids dad would come over. He was nice to me. Sometimes when he took the kids out he would even take me with them. I remember riding in the back of his blue pick up truck. He would take us to San Pedro for the day. Things were looking up! Maria and some of the people in her apartment complex knew me and were looking out for me. Sometimes a church bus would come by the apartments and pick up me and Maria's kids.

LIFE IN L.A.: ABANDONED

I knew better than to get too attached though. At the end of the day I was still another mouth to feed. After living with Maria and her kids for a few months at their apartment off of Mariposa and 8th, she told me I was going to have to stay somewhere else. *Here we go again*, I thought. But unlike the others, Maria didn't just put me out on the street. She had already been working on another place for me to stay.

Jorge was a friend of Maria's. He lived in another building right up from us on Mariposa. He seemed like a nice guy. I had met him before. He was in his late twenties, probably from El Salvador. He was in a wheelchair because he had been shot in a drive-by in the front of his apartment. He was partially paralyzed from his waist down. Jorge lived by himself and since he needed help he told Maria I should come live with him. So I moved down the street into Jorge's place.

I helped Jorge with whatever he needed, even with his physical therapy exercises. He was determined that he would build up enough of strength in his body to walk again. I helped him get to doctor appointments, pushing his wheel chair down sidewalks, helping him get on and off the metro. Obviously, he helped me by giving me a place to stay, feeding me even buying me some clothes. He never made me feel like I was a burden to him.

I don't know why, but I never fully believed that my parents were dead. I knew that if they were to come back to California for me they would go to the last place they left me. The whole time I was staying with Maria, at least once a week or so I would try to walk over to my old neighborhood around 7th and Magnolia, just so the people at the old apartment complex would know I was okay. I could also find out if anyone had seen my parents. A couple of times Jorge went with me. He even gave his phone number to a few of the people who knew my parents, just in case they came back. Things were the best they had been for me since my parents left. Between Maria, Jorge and some of the other people in the apartment complex, I actually had some clothes. I had food everyday and a safe place to sleep at night. To this day I am so grateful for them!

"Ten Cuidado," (be careful) Jorge said as I walked out the door. I told him I was going to go to my old neighborhood and would be back later.

I was playing with some of the kids in the parking lot behind the apartment building when someone ran down the stairs and shouted, "Juan your parents are here!" I took off running to the second floor. That's when I saw them. I saw my parents standing outside one of the neighbor's door talking to them.

"How are you doing son?" my dad asked in Spanish. My mom hugged me and in that one second I felt more joy, happiness, relief than I had probably felt in my whole life. All of a sudden I wasn't concerned with why they left me and why they had been gone for so long. *How long had they been gone anyway? Six months? Eight months? Close to a year?* It seemed like forever, but it didn't matter anymore. I was just glad they were there!

AT 8-YEARS-OLD, THE ONLY THING WORSE THAN BEING HIT WAS BEING HOMELESS. THERE HAD TO BE MORE TO LIFE THAN THIS!

Since my parents obviously didn't have a place to stay we walked back to Jorge's. The whole way there we talked. They asked questions about where I stayed and what I had been doing. I told them almost everything. Some things, like what happened to me in that dark alleyway, I never told them. What if I got in trouble for walking around? What if they thought it was my fault?

Jorge let my parents and sister come in and stay with us for a few nights. He talked to the apartment manager and within two or three days they had an apartment ready for my family to move into. The people in the apartment complex who knew me and had been watching out for me began helping my parents. Someone gave an extra set of sheets, someone else an extra chair, someone else a pot or a pan. Before long we had the basic things we needed.

The joy and relief I felt when I saw my parents standing on that metal walkway didn't last long. My dad continued his abusive patterns. He hit my mom and called her horrible names. It only took a few weeks before he started hitting me too. He slapped me in my face. He was so mean to me. Sometimes I wondered why he hated me so much. What had I ever done for him to hate me so much?

How had I forgotten this? How had I forgotten what life was like with them? I guess in my mind survival outweighed safety. At 8-years-old, the only thing worse than being hit was being homeless. There had to be more to life than this!

About a month or two later my dad was gone again. This time he was bringing a relative over for Jorge. He was only gone a few weeks. After everything Jorge had done for me I was glad my dad didn't just take his money and run.

One night after my dad came back from what became known as one of his "business trips" a couple of guys stormed into our apartment with a knife. They were after my dad, saying they were going to kill him. My mom, sister and I were crouched in the corner screaming as my dad grabbed a very large knife from a drawer and chased them out of our apartment. I'm not sure why they wanted to kill him, but he must have believed that they weren't going to leave him alone. We moved within a week.

Nobody ever really talked about my parents leaving me in L.A. Nobody talked about me living on the streets. Sometimes, it was as if it never even happened – but it did. I remember! I may not remember every single thing but I remember a lot! Still, today it is hard for me to communicate how that time in my life affected me. I do not like to think too deeply on it. I walk away with

NEVER ALONE

one conclusion. It is a miracle I came out of that alive!

CHAPTER

3

LIFE IN L.A.

Part 2: Father Figure

"See, I have engraved you on the palms of my hands; your walls are ever before me."
Isaiah 49:16 (NIV)

NEVER ALONE

We ended up moving just a few blocks away from Jorge. My dad landed a job as a property manager at some apartments. My parents re-enrolled me in school. Looking back it seems like I went right into third grade even though I had missed my entire second grade school year while I was on the streets.

It had been less than a year since they came back from Honduras. I remember this place because I took a pretty hard beating from my dad there. I was about 9-years-old. Something happened between him and my mom and he started beating her – hitting her in the face, grabbing her by her hair, kicking her, cursing her. Calling her everything you can imagine. She was bleeding. I was afraid he was going to kill her! I jumped on his back. "Get off of her!" I screamed as he began trying to pull me off. My mom ran to the bathroom and locked herself in. He finally pulled me off of his back and threw me on the floor kicking me in my stomach, my head, cussing me out and telling me what a piece of trash I was. All I could do was lay there and try to cover my head as he kept on kicking me. I must have eventually blacked out because when I woke up I was in the same spot on the floor and I could hear him talking to my mom.

"I'm sorry," he told her in Spanish. "I won't do it again," he said, trying to convince her to open the bathroom door. These kinds of episodes happened frequently, but this was the first time he had beaten me to the point that I blacked out.

At some point after that incident we left those apartments and moved to a place off of Dewey and Pico. My mom was pregnant. Things had calmed down for a bit. My dad was gone on one of his "business trips." My mom was getting pretty far along in her pregnancy. She was trying to keep food on the table for me and Johana. Sometimes it was there and sometimes it wasn't, but at least we weren't dealing with all of the beat downs from my dad.

LIFE IN L.A.: FATHER FIGURE

On May 22, 1994 my little brother Cristian was born. My dad was still gone, so some friends of my mom drove her to the hospital. Johana and I stayed behind. I was 10 when Cris was born. I remember he would cry and cry. Sometimes my mom just couldn't handle it anymore. She needed a break. I would take him from her and walk around with him trying to get him to sleep. I would lay Cris on my stomach and he would fall asleep. We slept like that a lot.

After Cris was born a man started coming around. He was so nice to me when my mom was around but when she walked away he would talk trash to me. I'm sure my mom was worried about food and making sure we had a place to live. My dad had been gone for several months and who knew how long it had been since the rent had been paid. Maybe that's why she ended up moving us in with this guy. I think he lived in the valley. We had never lived that far out of the city before.

I think Cristian was about 4-months-old when my dad came back and found us. He found some paperwork and tracked down my mom, talking her into meeting him. It was daytime when my mom, Johana, Cristian and I went to meet him in a park. Maybe my mom thought it would be safer to meet him in public. I watched my dad get out of a car. The person who drove him there stayed behind the wheel. This was the first time my dad ever saw Cristian. I watched Johana playing on the playground while keeping an eye on my mom. Mom and Dad were talking. I knew he was trying to convince her to come with him. She must have been telling him no because before I knew it he pulled a knife out and was pointing it in her stomach. The next thing I knew we were all in the car and just like that we were back with my dad.

I was almost eleven when we landed back in the city in an apartment building off of Arapahoe and San Marino. I have more memories of this place than the ones prior, probably because I was getting older. I had been enrolled in yet another school. I was in 4th grade going to my fourth elementary school. I felt a lot more comfortable speaking English by that time. I learned a

NEVER ALONE

lot of my English from listening to the radio or watching TV.

The apartment complex we lived in had a swimming pool in the courtyard and the apartments surrounded it, like you would see at a motel. As soon as you walked out of our apartment door there was a shared walkway with metal railing overlooking the pool. I became friends with a guy who lived on the other side of the pool from us. We lived on the third floor and he lived on the second floor. The apartment building was 3 floors high. He and I would go up to the roof on his side of the building and jump into the pool. That was a lot of fun!

I also remember going to a week-long camp with my school. One of my teachers paid for me to go. It was up in the mountains somewhere. I slept in a sleeping bag for the first time. I don't even know that I knew what a sleeping bag was before this. They set up military cots in a huge tent for us. Every morning we would go hiking and I learned how to shoot a bow and arrow. This is where I discovered that I loved nature and the outdoors. Away from the city life was so different. It was quite and peaceful. I almost felt safe. It was at this camp that I looked up one night and was completely surprised at how many stars were in the sky. It was beautiful! That was one of the best weeks of my life to that point. Not just because I was able to get away from home for a week but because I learned so much. Something I had often wondered about had been confirmed. There was more to life than I had experienced and knew.

Back home, on Arapahoe, the streets were run by gangs. My friends from the apartment complex and I were surrounded by them. It was while we lived here that I started running with gangs.

Not too long after my 5th grade year started we moved again. This time we moved to Atwater and yet again I had to switch schools. I hated it. I felt like an outsider. I started getting into a lot of fights. Four or five months later we moved again. School would have been out in about a month but we moved anyway. We moved to an area called Eagle Rock, off of Fletcher this time.

LIFE IN L.A.: FATHER FIGURE

This was the third school I had gone to for 5th grade alone. Only two things remained constant through moving. The neighborhoods were run by gangs and I didn't fit in anywhere at school. The only place I found to fit in was with the gangs. Maybe I didn't necessarily fit in, since I desired something different out of life, but they were the ones who made me feel accepted.

It was so frustrating moving constantly – leaving in the middle of the night because the rent hadn't been paid. Sometimes we had to start all over with nothing because we didn't have a way to move the furniture. I began to understand that if my dad would just work a real job and not take "business trips", we could pay the rent and quit moving.

One day during this time my dad left the house for a few hours. Immediately after my dad left my mom took a bag and walked out the door. I knew she was trying to leave him. My dad had just beaten her again. She just walked out and left me there with Johana and Cris. I ran after her. I followed her all the way down Fletcher crying and begging her not to leave us. "Mom, please don't leave us with him." I begged her in Spanish. She kept walking.

"Go back home Juan Pablo. You aren't coming with me." I followed her all the way to the bus stop at Fletcher and San Fernando. Nothing I said mattered. My crying and begging didn't faze her. I knew what he did to her, but she knew what he did to me too. How could she just leave us? How could she leave me again? I watched her get on the bus before I headed back to the apartment with Johana and Cris. She was gone for awhile when somehow my dad found her and made her come back.

We lived on Fletcher Drive for four or five months. By the time I started middle school we had moved again. This time we were off Marguerite Street. I was in 6th grade going to Irving Middle School. I don't know what my dad was thinking when he took me into the bedroom one day and sat me down. He said something to the effect that I was growing up into a man now and I needed to learn about the birds and the bees. He put porn on the TV and left

NEVER ALONE

the room. I look back now and wonder, *who does this? How do you just sit your 12- year-old down and put porn in their face?* He basically told me that porn was okay and everything they were doing was okay. Not only is that disgusting behavior out of a parent, but it is destructive for the child.

The longest I remember living anywhere was on Marguerite Street. I actually stayed in the same school for my 6th, 7th and 8th grade years – that is when I would actually go to school. Even with that bit of stability, I became very depressed while we lived here. My dad was gone on his "business trips" a lot.

If you haven't already figured out what I mean by "business trips" let me explain. My dad was a "coyote". A "coyote" is someone who brings people across the border into the United States illegally. When he left us to go on a "business trip" that is what he would do. He could be gone anywhere from a month to six months, maybe even up to eight or nine months at a time. His being away wasn't all that bad since when he was around he was so abusive.

As I got older, I started becoming angry. I was angry that because my dad wasn't around, my mom and me had to figure out how to eat and pay the rent. I was angry that when he was around he would beat us and say horrible things to us. I was angry that he would tell me what a piece of trash I was and how I would never be anything. *You tell me what a piece of trash I am and I'll never be anything but I've gotten pretty good at stealing and bringing in money so we wouldn't starve and be on the streets*, I would think to myself.

I wouldn't go to school for a few days at a time, sometimes even a week at a time, so I could make some money. I remember working a job for a contractor. For two days I worked my butt off. By this time I was around 13 or 14-years-old. At the end of the second day the job was done, however, the guy wouldn't pay me what he owed me. I became so angry that I began yelling, cussing and tearing up his job site. He ended up paying me just to get me out of there.

LIFE IN L.A.: FATHER FIGURE

The fast money came from stealing. I stole bikes, roller blades, CD's. I wore cargo pants and put five or six CD's down each of the side pockets. I had a system for getting the bikes and roller blades out of the stores I would hit. The guy who drove the ice cream truck in our neighborhood was my buyer. "What did you get today?" he would ask me in Spanish. He mainly bought the bikes and roller blades. I would sell the CD's on the street or at school. I gave the majority of the money to my mom and kept $10 or $20 for myself. I don't ever remember her asking me where the money came from.

> **I WAS STILL HANGING OUT WITH GANGS AND BY THIS TIME, I HAD STARTED RUNNING DRUGS FOR THEM.**

I was still hanging out with gangs and by this time, I had started running drugs for them. That was fast money too, but I wasn't sure how much I wanted to do that. The more I wanted that quick cash the more they would want from me. At some point I would have to decide. When I was in 7th grade I was jumped into a well-known gang and I began spending more time with my new "family". However, this was a lot more than running drugs. I saw things that I hated! I saw things that scared me! Even though I tried to play tough on the outside, this stuff made me sick.

Every boy needs a man to encourage them, protect them, teach them – to be there for them. Everyone needs to feel wanted and to have someone to build you up and not tear you down. Every boy needs a *Father Figure*. I wanted that. I had a couple of teachers at school who influenced me a lot, Mr. Florez and Mr. Nelson. Somehow, what they said got through my anger and depression. Somehow, what they said got through my tough exterior and my hard heart. Somehow, what they said made sense in my mind. "If you want to change yourself, surround yourself with good people." They would talk to me and

NEVER ALONE

encourage me. They cared about me and knew I could do much better than I was doing. They believed in me!

Before long, I began spending more and more time at home. I wasn't hanging out as much with my crew.

"Come on Juan," they would say.

"I can't. I have to help with my little sister and brother today."

At some point towards the end of my 8th grade year my dad let me take the car out and drive it. I was 14 – and no, I didn't have any type of license, but I had been driving off and on for a few years now. While I was driving the transmission went out. The only direction the car would move was in reverse. *Great*, I thought to myself as I'm driving backwards down the street, *he's going to beat the crap out of me*. I was literally a block from home when I passed a cop. I was sure a car going backwards down the street looked suspicious. Sure enough, he turned around and pulled me over.

"I ain't no banger," I said in Spanish as I put both my hands out of the window. I explained to the officers what was wrong with the car. They asked for my license so I lied. I told them that I had taken the test for my driver's license and was waiting on it to come in the mail. So one of the officers decided to drive the car backwards around the corner to our place on Marguerite Street. I rode in handcuffs in the patrol car. Luckily for me, telling the truth wasn't a big deal in my house, so my dad went along with my story to the police officers.

They let me go, but for some reason one of the officers took an interest in me. He would stop by every so often to check on me and one day he brought me some information about a magnet high school that specialized in law enforcement. This opportunity would take me to a new school – away from where my current friends were going. *Could this be the break I needed? Could this be how I could change myself – by surrounding myself with good people?*

I don't think I had ever been so excited in my whole life when I found out

LIFE IN L.A.: FATHER FIGURE

that I had been accepted into the magnet school, especially because by being accepted I had proven my dad wrong. He told me I would never make it into the program.

The school was on the other side of the city, so I would need to get up very early to make all of the bus connections. I wouldn't get home until late, but that was okay with me. I wanted to go to this school. It was my ticket away from the life I had been exposed to (even if it was just Monday through Friday). It was my ticket to more in life. It was my ticket to better myself. It was my ticket to having a future with a real job- even a career.

I loved the magnet program! I was so thankful for this opportunity! I had been in the program almost one semester when my world was once again turned upside down. This time I was given a ticket I wanted no part of, but I had no choice.

CHAPTER

2,066 MILES

"And you have not delivered me into the hand of the enemy; You have set my feet in a broad place."
Psalm 31:8 (ESV)

NEVER ALONE

It was a rainy day in December when we pulled up to the Greyhound Bus station in Glendale, CA. I remember so clearly driving around a circle to be dropped off at the door of the bus stop. The architecture resembled more of a cathedral type building than a Greyhound Station. Earlier that morning we loaded our bags, which had everything we owned in them, into our car. We drove to my parent's friend's house so that they could drop us off at the bus station. It was just a few months ago that my dad had started talking about us moving to another state. This time we were on a bus headed for Indianapolis, IN.

"There's jobs there. It's safer too," my dad said.

Moving was normal for us. We had moved about a month ago from Marguerite Street. Since coming to the U.S., I can remember living in about fourteen different places, but leaving California and taking us across the country – that was new.

Why do we always have to move around? Why can't we just stay put? I just want to finish school where I am! I thought to myself. *I'm actually doing good in school and enjoying it. I could actually have a future and now they have to go and ruin it.* In my mind these were good arguments, but I knew better than to argue with him. If this is what he wanted to do, no one could talk him out of it.

A few weeks prior to the big move, my parents began selling all of our stuff. Eventually basically all we owned were our clothes and we didn't have a lot of those. I don't even remember going to school for several days leading up to the move. For a few days, maybe even weeks, we slept on the floor because the couches and mattresses we previously slept on were sold. Anything we couldn't fit into a duffel bag was eventually gone. One day I finally got up enough of courage to ask them.

"Please let me stay!" Of course their response was no. What was I thinking asking such a question, let alone hoping that they would let me stay behind? I was the translator for the family. They needed me.

2,066 MILES

I stared out the window that morning as we made our way out of the city and drove through the streets I called home. Life had been hard and rough in the streets of west L.A., but they were home to me and all I had known for the last 10 years. On December 10, 1999 my mom, dad, brother, sister and I got on a bus to travel 2,066 miles across the country. We were starting a new life in Indianapolis, IN. I hated every mile of it.

> **WE WERE TOTALLY ON OUR OWN AND AT THE MERCY OF COMPLETE STRANGERS.**

I don't remember a lot about the ride for those 2,066 miles other than the bus made a lot of stops, the seats had some crazy pattern from the 80's on them and I slept and looked out the window – a lot. I do remember we came to a place in our journey where there was snow on the ground. I was about one month away from turning 16 and it was the first time I had ever seen snow. The next evening after dark sometime, we finally made it to Indianapolis. We drove past the zoo, which was all lit up with Christmas lights. Once we got off of the bus and got all of our bags we were able to find a Comfort Inn® not too far away. I don't think I've mentioned that we knew absolutely NO ONE in Indianapolis. We were totally on our own and at the mercy of complete strangers. My dad paid for one or two nights with the cash that he'd gotten from selling our stuff in Los Angeles.

The next day was a Sunday. My mom and siblings stayed in the room while my dad and I went to the lobby to get breakfast. There was some commotion in the lobby between a private investigator from Mexico and some police officers. The private investigator was trying to explain to the officers what happened to him the night before. His arm was all bandaged up and it looked pretty bad. Everyone in that circle was having a hard time communicating because the private investigator didn't speak English and the

NEVER ALONE

police officers didn't speak Spanish. Before I knew it, I was pulled into the middle of the discussion, translating for both sides.

The private investigator had been hired by a family in Mexico to find their runaway son-in-law who fled to Indianapolis. The family was desperate to bring the son-in-law back to Mexico, as he had murdered their daughter and their grandchildren. The private investigator actually found the son-in-law the night before and there had been an altercation. The fugitive tried to cut the private investigator's arm off and almost succeeded. (I'm not kidding – I can't even make this stuff up!)

Once I was done translating for this bizarre scene, my dad and I left the hotel and walked around the city. We came to the RCA Dome where the Colts and Patriots were playing. We walked right in like we belonged there and actually watched a quarter of the game before leaving to go back to the hotel.

The next morning we went out again to walk around and see more of the city. This time my dad let my mom, Johana and Cristian come along. We came across a Catholic Church and walked in because my dad wanted to ask them for help. There was a priest who spoke Spanish there, so I didn't have to translate this time. My dad began giving them this very sad story, which was also a lie. He went on about how we rode here on a bus all the way from Los Angeles and someone had robbed us and stolen all our money. He told the priest we had no money and nowhere to stay. The priest gave my dad his contact information so that he could stay in touch and we walked back to the hotel.

We woke up the following morning to someone from the front desk knocking on our door, asking why we hadn't paid for the night before. This time I had to be the translator, telling the hotel that we had been robbed and had no money, but we were getting help from the church and they would pay for it. My dad went back to the church and told the priest that the hotel was going to kick us out on the street if we didn't get the bill paid, so the church ended up paying for us to stay about another week.

It was getting close to Christmas and we ended up going to Mass one evening. The priest recognized us in the congregation. He asked our family to stand and he began to tell the parishioners that we were a family in need. He took up a collection for us that evening and gave the money to my parents. My dad stayed in communication with the church and within a few days, the priest picked us up from the hotel and took us to a shelter that would accept our family.

We spent Christmas and New Year (Y2K) at the shelter. We were there almost a month, I think. My parents, brother, sister and I slept in a small room together. For the most part the people running it were pretty nice and they fed us a couple meals a day. There were probably around 30 people staying there at the time. We were the only Spanish speaking family. There were some single moms with kids and single dads with kids. We were the only family in the shelter with both a mom and a dad.

From time to time my parents would let me go out by myself. I found a basketball court not far away from the shelter and I hung out there sometimes. Other times I would just walk around downtown and go to the mall there. One day I walked into one of the department stores and asked to see some of the watches. I asked to see three or four of the nice Fossil® watches. The sales lady that was helping me got distracted with another customer and walked away. I laid all of the watches back on the counter except for one. I pulled my shirt down over my wrist and walked out. I walked back towards the shelter, found a convenience store and sold the watch for $60. I knew we needed money and at some point I would need to give it to my parents. They never once questioned how I would come up with money.

At one point we met a businessman who sometimes had small jobs my dad and I could work to help give us extra cash. One time we painted an office

NEVER ALONE

for him. I had never painted before. When we were finished it looked horrible, but he didn't complain and he still paid us for the days work. We called him Mr. Paul. Mr. Paul even picked up our whole family from the shelter and took us to his house on the other side of town for Christmas dinner. He drove a Range Rover and his house was beautiful. We had dinner with him, his wife and kids. They even gave us some gifts before taking us back to the shelter. We had a curfew at the shelter. If we weren't back by 10 p.m. we couldn't get back in for the night.

After a few more weeks at the shelter, the priest and Mr. Paul helped us find our own place to live on the south side of Indianapolis. The shelter gave us furniture, the priest gave us money for rent and utilities and Mr. Paul gave us a car. We had been in Indianapolis a little over a month and because of their help we were able to start a new life.

Starting a new life in Indianapolis meant finding a new school. The new high school in Indiana did not recognize the magnet school I had come from in California. I had worked so hard to get into that program. These people were telling me that everything I had done for the last year wasn't good enough for them. They made me completely start over as a freshman.

Are you serious? I was angry, frustrated and humiliated. I would be almost 20-years-old before I could graduate. To make matters worse I was harassed and beat up by kids claiming to be KKK at my new school. I was told that "my kind" wasn't wanted there. Yeah, well I didn't want to be there just as bad as they didn't want me there.

School became very difficult for me. I went from making decent grades in California to flunking most of my classes at my new school in Indiana. By moving around and missing so much school when I was younger, I never learned how to read or write English properly. I guess that was to be expected since I hadn't gone to kindergarten or second grade. I had gone to six different elementary schools for the grades I did complete. I mixed Spanish

2,066 MILES

into everything. In California it hadn't been a big deal. Early on, I was able to use Spanish in my classes. After that most everyone in our school knew Spanish too, so they knew what I was saying or writing. That was not the case at my new school. I hated it. The only thing I looked forward to was playing soccer and hanging out with a group of guys who had included me in their circle.

Springtime approached and my parents still weren't working real jobs. My dad had gotten some information that soccer refs were needed for some Hispanic leagues around Indianapolis, so he and I would go and ref on Saturdays and Sundays. The money we were paid from reffing got us through from one week to the next. Sometimes he might let me keep $5 or $10 of it.

My mom really wanted to go to work. "That's why we moved here right, because there are jobs? Why aren't we working," she would ask him. She finally convinced him to let her start applying for jobs.

Even though we were making it week to week, my dad was still my dad. Lying, conning and taking whatever people would give him. He regularly beat my mom when she didn't do what he said and yelled at me and my sister, putting his hands on us. He would cuss us out like we weren't even his own kids. At this point life looked horrible. Once I even tried to run away and go back to California. I made it to the airport. I was just sitting there when the cops found me. My parents had reported me missing and the cops took me back home.

Eventually, I discovered that there was more to our leaving California than simply finding better jobs and a safer place to live. We left because my dad crossed the wrong people and they wanted to hurt him.

2,066 Miles for this? *2,066 Miles* to be flunking out of school and still be four years away from graduating. *2,066 Miles* for people to hate you for your skin color. *2,066 Miles* so you can work all weekend and give the money to your parents because your dad won't hold down a real job. *2,066 Miles* so you

51

NEVER ALONE

can keep being cussed out, beat up and told you're nothing and never will be by your dad.

At first, all I could see was that those *2,066 Miles* were the worst thing that ever happened to me. In my mind, I would have been better off alone. I didn't realize that in reality, God orchestrated this move and had actually set my feet in a broad place!

CHAPTER

5

TURNING POINT

"And everyone who calls on the name of the Lord will be saved."
Acts 2:21 (NIV)

NEVER ALONE

Over the next few months we settled into our new life in a little town right outside of Indianapolis. My brother, sister and I were going to school and my parents were applying for jobs. If they were called back for interviews I would go with them and translate. They both ended up getting a job at a hotel about 10 minutes from where we lived. My mom worked in housekeeping and my dad worked in laundry. They worked the same days and hours, which was great for my dad, so he could keep an eye on my mom while making some money too.

He always had an issue with one thing or another at work. One day he wanted me to go into the hotel and translate for him to one of the managers. The manager I spoke with that day was Liz. She was young and had long blonde curly hair – and she was cute. When my parents suggested that I work at the hotel after school to help bring in more money, I thought it was a great idea. Not because I wanted to give them money, but because it would allow me to see Liz more often.

We began talking and seeing each other outside of work and within a couple of months we were inseparable. There was something different about her. I loved spending time with her not to mention it got me away from the reality of my home life. My parents didn't mind the time I spent with her either. Not because they were enjoying my happiness. My dad wanted her to get close to our family so that he could get money out of her. "Don't trust them," I told her. "He's going to end up asking you for money and he'll never pay you back."

Liz grew up very differently than I had. She didn't believe that my dad would take advantage of her. She thought I just had some issues with my parents, but I couldn't tell her everything that had happened. I couldn't tell her everything I had been through or what our family life was actually like. I really cared for her and didn't want her to run the opposite direction.

TURNING POINT

My past and my family life wasn't the only thing I was keeping from her. I was younger than she thought. When I filled out the application to work at the hotel, my dad had me lie about some of the information. Liz thought I was 18 when I was actually 16. I let her believe that for a while, until I found out that she had a 3-year-old son. I thought that would be the perfect time to come clean about my age. "I knew some things didn't make sense," she said "but I wouldn't have thought you were 16." Liz was uncomfortable with our age difference, but I wasn't your typical 16-year-old. I had been through more and seen more than your average 40-year-old. We continued to talk and spend time with each other.

"I've got a lot of things I have to get right in my life," she would say. "I have to get back in church and live right. I have to raise Nate in church. If we're going to be together you have to come to church with us."

Okay, I thought. *It can't hurt anything. It's just church.*

Over the next several months Liz and I continued dating. We would go to church together with Nate. During the church service when there was singing or at the end when the pastor spoke, she would just cry. I didn't understand why she wanted to go to church if all she was going to do was cry. "Seriously, how does this make you feel better?" I would ask her. Sometimes, she would go to the front of the church and people would stand around her and pray for her and she would just cry and cry and cry. I didn't realize until much later that she needed God to help her with some things inside that hurt her so deeply. She knew she had made decisions in her life that dishonored God and she felt badly about them. I didn't understand why the whole church thing was necessary. I just knew there was something about her that I loved and I would do anything for her.

"Why are you with me?" I would ask her. "I don't have anything to really offer you or Nate."

"I know when people look at us it doesn't make sense," Liz said. "Our

NEVER ALONE

backgrounds are completely different and I'm a little bit older than you, but there is something inside of you that I can't explain. There is so much potential! You are so much more than people think you are."

Even after knowing Liz for only four or five months, I knew I wanted to spend the rest of my life with her. I knew I wanted to marry her and be a dad to Nate, especially since his biological father was nowhere in the picture. I loved them! Even Liz had a hard time believing me when I asked her to marry me. "Are you serious?" she asked me. I was more serious about spending my life with her than anything else in the world.

In my short life I had seen a lot of things that made me know what I didn't want for my life, but it also made me aware of what I did want. She said yes to me and from that moment on we began to work towards setting things right in our own lives that would move us closer to being able to get married. We were both young, but my turning 18 and my schooling were our biggest obstacles. Turning 18 would come in about a year, but school was an entirely separate issue. I was so far behind from the move. Not to mention school was so much harder that I fell that much further behind. It's so frustrating when you look stupid because you can't just open a book and figure something out on your own. Liz tried to help me as much as she could, but I still felt like I was drowning in school.

It was May of 2001 and school had just let out for the summer. I had just come home from spending some time with Liz and Nate and I could tell that my dad was in one of his moods. He started trying to argue with me. I tried to ignore him but he kept getting in my face. Before I knew it he had taken a metal pole that was kept in the corner of our living room and began to hit me with it and cuss me out. He kept whipping the metal bar over my back as I raised my arms over my head, trying to protect myself. Johana and Cristian were screaming for him to stop. My mom was trying to stop him but he just kept going at it. Just as he brought the pole up in the air to bring it back down on me I was able to get out from underneath it. I crawled around on the floor

TURNING POINT

and grabbed him from behind, holding both of his arms down while yelling at my mom to call the cops. Not once did I hit him. Not because he didn't deserve it, but because he was still my dad.

I held him down until the cops got there so he couldn't hit me with the pole anymore. The whole time he's yelling, cussing and trying to get loose. I knew if I let him go he would go crazy on me. I finally let him go when the cops got there. He denied hitting me with anything even though I had bruises and scratches on my back, arms and around my neck. When the cops questioned my mom she also told them that he hadn't hit me – that we were just arguing. Both of them told the cops I was being your typical disrespectful teenager. This didn't surprise me. She was afraid of him. The cops ordered me to go back into the house, but I wasn't going back into that house. I knew that if I did, either me or my dad would end up getting hurt badly or even worse.

"If you don't go back into the house, you're going to jail," the officer told me.

"Then take me to jail. I'm not going back in there," I replied. They ended up letting me leave only because my mom told them it was okay. She knew what would happen if I went back in. He had put his hands on me for the last time. I moved out that night and never went back. I was 17-years-old. I'm sure my mom thought I would stay gone for a few weeks and come back home just like she used to do when we lived in California, but I was done! I was done being beat on and told that I would never be anything. I was done with never knowing when my dad would go crazy on us. And I was done pretending. He had gotten away with it for too long. I could no longer pretend that he was innocent or that it was okay to beat us and talk to us like dirt.

I got a job at a tire company and worked that entire summer. I didn't go back to high school. I'm not proud of that! It has bothered me a lot in my life. In fact I would tell anyone that quitting school is not an option, but there were so many obstacles. So many areas of my life that I had little to no control over affected my education. It's not like I didn't have a desire to learn, because I did! I dreamed of being a doctor or even a pilot, but I was almost 18 years old. I didn't want to be finishing school when I was 20 or 21.

I worked hard at my job and worked my way up. I was proud of myself. I didn't mind hard work. I knew by my not having a high school diploma that working hard would be the only way I would make anything of myself. Liz and I were still together and wanted to get married. Things were good – except for when we went to church. I still didn't understand the purpose of going if all you were going to do was cry. I didn't know all the things that weighed on Liz's heart and mind and she didn't know all the things that weighed on me. I don't think I felt sorry for myself because of what I had been through, everyone goes through stuff, but I had so much anger inside. Anger, because a lot of the things I went through didn't have to happen if my parents would have made different choices.

I may not have participated in worship or went to the altar for prayer when we went to church, but I paid attention to what was being said. I wasn't just angry because Liz cried every time we went to church. I was angry because I heard it said over and over that I needed to believe that God was good, but people had no idea what I had been through. They wanted me to believe that He loved me and wanted the best for me.

Are you kidding me? How does He want the best for me? If He is really God and knows everything how did He miss me being alone on the streets? How did He miss me being told that my parents were dead? How did He miss me being beaten and kicked in the head by my dad? How is that "wanting the best for me"? I'm not sure why but, He definitely doesn't love me. Maybe, He loves others but, definitely not me.

After several months, maybe even a year of going to church with Liz, something started to shift inside of me. I began to grow tired of feeling the way I did on the inside. I was tired of being angry. One night the message was about being tired of situations in your life. I was tired! I was tired of not being

TURNING POINT

where I wanted to be in life. I was tired of carrying around the baggage of all that had happened in my life. I was tired of how it all weighed on my mind. During altar call – the part of the service where people walk forward to pray – I got out of my seat and walked to the altar with tears running down my face. I asked Jesus to save me and to help me. I received Him as my Lord and Savior.

I don't know how to explain to you what happened exactly. It was like the anger was taken away from me. For the first time in my life I felt peace. For the first time in my life I felt like everything was going to be okay. Receiving Christ was my *Turning Point*. My past was still my past. The things that had happened to me and the things I had done myself weren't taken away, but I began to see and understand that God really was good! I began to see that it was only a miracle that I was even still alive! He had brought me to this place in my life where I understood that if it weren't for Him, I would not be here! He really did love me and had spared my life many times!

WHEN I GAVE MY HEART TO JESUS AND DECIDED TO LIVE MY LIFE FOR HIM, I REALLY WAS ALL IN.

When I gave my heart to Jesus and decided to live my life for Him, I really was all in. I didn't want to pretend I was something that I really wasn't. It was still a process. I still had to change a lot about myself. I had to walk-out my salvation as I learned and grew in my relationship with Jesus. I had a lot to learn and quite frankly I was a young man who thought I knew everything because of what I had been through.

On February 2, 2002, just 11 days after my 18th birthday Liz and I were married. We had a very small ceremony at our church. Only our immediate family joined us as the associate pastor of the church performed our ceremony. We had dreams of a big, beautiful, fancy wedding. Our little ceremony was quite the opposite, but that is not what was important. We

NEVER ALONE

made a vow before God to each other that day, a vow that no matter what, we would finish this life together.

I wish I could tell you it's been so easy and that we've danced through the tulips the whole time, but that would be a lie. There have been a lot of rough times. My *Turning Point* of salvation didn't exclude me from future hardships, frustration, disappointments and pain. Even though I had already been through what I would consider my fair share, there were seasons ahead of me that I only got through because I learned how to depend on God to get me through them. There were times I wanted to quit, but as my Pastor says, "you can think about quitting as long as you know you won't." My *Turning Point* didn't promise a future without difficulty and pain, but it did promise that because of Jesus Christ I had everything I needed, not just to get through, but to overcome every situation I would face.

God tells us in John 16:33, "I have said these things to you, that in me you may have peace. In the world you will have tribulation. But take heart; I have overcome the world." He is so good to remind us in His Word that we will have tribulation in this world. Tribulation can be trouble, suffering, distress, misery, unhappiness, sadness, grief, sorrow, pain, anguish, agony, adversity, worry, hardship, affliction or tragedy. As long as we live in this world we will experience tribulation, and more than likely, we will experience it several times. God tells us it's going to happen, but once we receive Him into our heart, He promises peace! Peace that doesn't make sense in a world full of tribulation.

Let's pause a moment here. I want to take a break from sharing how my life has unfolded chronologically.

There are things that I can't explain. I can't tell you why they happened. All I know is that God is still there through them and we have a choice to come out bitter or better, weaker or stronger. These truths are so important, that I'm going to take a break in my story, to share with you how God revealed

TURNING POINT

these truths through some of our family trials.

I don't know why after a healthy pregnancy our third son, Alex, was born with laryngomalacia. The tissues over his larynx were softened which allowed them to flop over his airway randomly. This caused him to have apnea moments. For example, his airway would suddenly become blocked and he couldn't get oxygen or during a feeding his milk would go down the wrong way and he would choke. Because his birth weight was good and he was still growing, the doctors thought that it was a mild form of laryngomalacia and that he would grow out of it.

When Alex was about a month old, Liz took him to a local children's hospital for a bronchoscopy. By the time they had gotten back home from the procedure there was a message on the home phone to call the hospital immediately. They told her that the doctor had already read the report and that she was to bring Alex straight back to the hospital. His case was much more severe than initially thought. Liz called me at work and told me to get to the hospital. Before I could get there they already had Alex on oxygen and hooked up to several monitors so they could do a sleep study on him. They were trying to figure out how many apneas he was having during his sleep and for how long. In another room they were teaching Liz how to do infant CPR. It was completely overwhelming!

Within a matter of hours our life completely changed. Alex was sent home with oxygen and apnea monitors that he was required to use 24 hours a day until further notice. The doctors advised us against putting Alex in any type of daycare environment. His respiratory system simply wouldn't be able to handle all the germs and viruses he could be exposed to in that setting. "He will be in the hospital every week if he is exposed to a lot," the doctor told us.

Within a day or two Liz and I made the decision that she would not return to work from her maternity leave. She would now stay home and care for Alex. Basically, overnight we went from a two-income household down to

NEVER ALONE

one. We didn't know how we were going to make it, especially with a family of seven, but if I had been able to provide everything for my family I would have never been able to watch God provide and care for us! He kept us and showed me that He is my provider!

The doctors recommended surgery for Alex. There was a chance he could outgrow this condition in a few years, but they were uncomfortable with the amount of Alex's apneas. "They aren't cutting him open!" I told Liz. "We're going to take care of him and pray for God to heal him!" For months the living room of our tiny house was set up with all of Alex's medical equipment. One of us slept downstairs with him every night and when one of the alarms on the apnea monitor went off, we jumped up and rubbed his back to help him get his breathing back on track. It was exhausting.

Some nights it seemed those alarms never stopped going off, and then they went off less and then even less, until some nights we would wake up and make sure the monitor was working because it hadn't gone off at all. When we checked the monitor, it was working – Alex just hadn't had an apnea that night. When Alex was 6-months-old the doctors took him off of everything! It was over! He was healed! I don't like that my son was sick. It scared Liz and I terribly, but if that hadn't happened I would have never known God as Healer! I would have never learned that I could trust Him to take care of my children.

In 2012 Liz suffered a miscarriage. That completely took us off guard. After being blessed to have four healthy pregnancies losing this child devastated us. That day and the events surrounding it are forever seared into our memory. I will never forget the look on Liz's face when she came out of the bathroom that afternoon. The kids had a day off of school and we had taken them out to a museum.

"Somethings not right," she told me with tears rolling down her cheeks. The doctor called us in for an ultrasound and sure enough...no heartbeat.

TURNING POINT

Just in case, Liz had blood work done every day for about three days. Her hormone levels were going down. We had lost the baby. My birthday was just a few days away and our 10-year wedding anniversary just two weeks away. Liz was still in her first trimester, but we loved and wanted this child.

"What did I do wrong," she would ask. "I don't understand why God wouldn't let us raise this child." I watched my wife grieve in hopelessness. To be honest, I was broken inside too. I had never felt this kind of pain but I had to be strong for Liz and our kids. I wasn't the greatest at communicating how I was feeling or what was going on inside of me, but a close friend of Liz's told me to make Liz talk about it. She told me that I needed to make Liz talk about what she is thinking and feeling and to not to let her keep this bottled up inside. For the most part I was able to get her to share what she was going through.

For weeks maybe even a few months we had a conversation daily or every other day about our baby that we now call Angel. It not only helped Liz, but it helped me. I was able to open up to Liz and tell her how much I wanted and loved this child and how disappointed I was that we couldn't keep him. It hurt me just as bad as it had hurt her. When she realized that it was almost like a weight had been taken off of her. She realized that she wasn't the only one bearing the grief. We knew we were walking this together.

Five years have gone since we lost Baby Angel. I still can't explain to you why it happened. What I can tell you is that without this trial or tribulation, I would have never experienced God's sweet presence overwhelm and heal my heart. I would have never depended on Him to help me be more sensitive toward my wife. Without God I would have never felt comfortable enough to be so vulnerable with my wife and share with her my feelings of losing our baby. Without God I wouldn't have the confidence that one day we will hold our child. We never got to hold Angel, but our hearts held him and still does. Just like I've never seen God physically hold me, but I have felt Him and I have seen the outcomes of situations that He has helped me with.

NEVER ALONE

How do we know if we are coming through tribulation the right way? It's simple – if our faith and trust in God is increasing then we are coming through tribulation the right way. The amount of tribulation or level of difficulty it brings isn't as important as our faith and trust in Jesus! Are we growing? Are we becoming more dependent on Him? Are we becoming more like Him?

My *Turning Point*, my decision to receive Christ as my Savior has changed everything! I am not perfect! I am still growing and learning how to be the "Real Me". The "Real Me" is who He has created me to be! I'm still working on being a better man, husband, father, brother and friend. Some days I get it right and some days I don't. I'm so thankful that He forgives me when I mess up and guides me as I try to lead my family. I'm thankful that His mercy is new every morning! I'm thankful for everything in my life that led up to my *Turning Point*! I'm thankful for my *Turning Point*! I'm thankful for everything He has helped me with, taken me through and shown me, not only about myself, but about Him since my *Turning Point*! I believe we all reach a place in life where we not only need, but want a *Turning Point*. Have you reached that place? Have you reached your *Turning Point*?

CHAPTER

6

MY BROTHER'S KEEPER

Part 1: Family of Five

"But he said to me, 'My grace is sufficient for you...'"

2 Corinthians 12:9 (NIV)

NEVER ALONE

It was December 2002. As I made my way to my mom's house that Friday evening, I knew something wasn't quite right.

"I need you to come to the house when you get off work today," my mom had said when she called me earlier. "I need to talk to you."

"What's going on?" I asked.

"I need to talk to you face to face," she said.

In my heart, I knew what was about to happen. My mom and I hadn't been on the best terms for several months now for several reasons. Among them, she wasn't happy that I had gotten married. Also, when I would try to give her advice regarding my younger brother and sister, it didn't go over well.

She was basically a single mom since my dad had been gone on one of his "business trips" for over a year at that point. Liz and I dropped him off at the Indianapolis International Airport the previous September to take his trip and we hadn't seen him since. I knew it was hard for her but it seemed like she didn't want any of my help. She definitely didn't want my advice. I had been telling her for months to switch her shift at work.

"The kids can't keep being left alone every evening," I would tell her. She worked second shift and I was trying to get her to go back to first shift. She was gone everyday when they came home from school and they were asleep by the time she got home at night. It wasn't a good situation. Johana had just turned 14 and Cris was 8 and this had been going on for several months now.

So Liz, Nate and I walked into my mom's apartment. Sending the kids to the back room, she took Liz and I up to the front room where just two months earlier we had celebrated Johana's 14th birthday and watched her open gifts. My mom began to tell me all that was going on. The kids weren't doing as they should. They were misbehaving, having other kids to the house while she was working and even going out at night. They were doing whatever they wanted. The neighbors had been watching and telling my mom everything.

MY BROTHER'S KEEPER: FAMILY OF FIVE

"This is why I told you to switch your shift!" I said. "What did you expect to happen? They are kids and they aren't being supervised!" Our conversation kept going back and forth in Spanish and started to get heated. I was getting frustrated that she hadn't done what I had been telling her to do and she was frustrated because I was trying to tell her what to do. Liz was sitting there watching it all unfold as I'm translating bits and pieces into English. And then it happens; my mom tells me in Spanish why I'm there. I just looked at her.

"What did she just say?" Liz asked, breaking the silence.

"She said that she can't handle the kids anymore and if we don't take them that she will put them in foster care." I translated.

"Bring them in," I said to my mom. "Tell them they have to come live with me." I knew she wasn't bluffing. She wasn't just trying to scare the kids into acting right. I knew she was serious. There was a pattern.

Anytime she came to a place where she couldn't handle things and life was too much for her, she would leave. Back in California she ran away from my dad so many times because he beat her. I got that, but I also knew the pattern. Life was becoming overwhelming for her and something had to change.

I just wanted to get the kids stuff and get out of there. I was so mad – so frustrated. *Why couldn't she just change her shift and be there to take care of them in the evening?* It seemed so simple to me. I knew there had to be more to it than the excuse that she just couldn't afford to go to first shift.

"Yeah, they can stay with us for a few weeks," Liz said. "They are on Christmas break anyway. Maybe your mom just needs a break." I didn't understand how Liz wasn't getting it. They were coming to live with us – not to visit or vacation.

"You don't understand," I told her. "She doesn't want them. If I don't take them they are going into foster care."

NEVER ALONE

"Well, why don't we keep them over the break. Before it's time for school to start, we'll talk again and go from there," she said. "I'm sure your mom just needs a break."

I looked at Liz in disbelief. What was she not understanding? I wasn't taking into account that my family was something very different than what she had always known. Her only life experience was that when you have a kid, you raise and take care of that kid. She hadn't come from where I came from. She had never been abandoned and didn't have siblings that had been raised in an orphanage.

"Fine," I said to my mom. "Get the kids." We yelled for them to come into the front room. I don't remember whether it was my mom or myself who told them they were coming to live with me. I just remember Cristian crying and my mom telling him it was Johana's fault.

"Come on get your stuff," I told them. "We need to go." The kids didn't have that much anyway. We walked out into the bitter-cold air and I loaded their backpacks in the trunk of our two-door Chrysler Sebring.

There was so much going through my mind on that drive back to the west side of town where we lived. Johana and Cris couldn't believe what just happened. Cris was crying and sobbing because he wanted his mom.

"It's okay, it's only for a few weeks Cristian," Liz said, trying to console him as Johana glared at her. She was angry. At this same time, my mom was taking care of a friend's daughter who was Johana's age. Johana didn't understand how my mom wouldn't let her own children live with her, but this girl could stay.

I wanted to scream at Liz and tell her to quit being in denial. I wanted to tell her to quit sugarcoating it. The kids were moving in with us and the sooner she understood that, the better, but the last thing I needed was to argue with her. We had three kids in the back seat and it was a week before Christmas. I had to figure things out.

MY BROTHER'S KEEPER: FAMILY OF FIVE

We had one extra room for them to sleep in, but we didn't have extra beds. How were we going to afford this? Liz and I both worked full time jobs with one kid in the house and we were making it paycheck to paycheck. How were we going to handle the extra expense of two more kids?

We got home, got the kids stuff unloaded and I went to the spare room to clean and set up the air mattress. That would have to do for now. Liz asked Cristian if he wanted to stay in Nate's room or in the spare room with Johana. He chose Johana.

JUST LIKE THAT, OVERNIGHT, WE WENT FROM A FAMILY OF THREE TO A FAMILY OF FIVE.

Once again I felt like the world was on my shoulders. Once again I felt responsible for everyone. Just like that, overnight, we went from a family of three to a *Family of Five*.

The next few days and weeks were hard. I was frustrated with my mom and my little sister and brother. I was mad at everyone. Johana was mad at the world and didn't want to be anywhere around us. Cristian would get so upset he would vomit. They had practically been raising themselves and doing whatever they wanted and now they were with Liz and I. Even though we didn't know how to raise them, we did have rules and they weren't used to that. I wasn't even 19-years-old yet! Liz and I had only been married 10 months. We had only lived in our home three months and quite frankly we were still trying to figure out how to be married and be a family with Nate.

I was a different person, or at least I was trying to be different. I wasn't the same person that I was when I lived with my parents. I had given my heart to the Lord and was still learning how to live differently than I used to. I didn't come from a Christian home and neither did Cris and Johana. Yet, here we were under the same roof again. Once again I am trying to take care of them. They wanted me to be their brother, but I couldn't. I had to be their father. Being their brother would have been much easier, but they needed guidance and direction. They needed someone to believe in them and not give up on them. They needed a father. I couldn't be who I used to be. Everyone in that house needed me to be who God had created me to be!

A few days before Christmas break was over and the kids would be going back to school, I began to talk to Liz. I wanted to prepare her. We needed to enroll the kids in the school district where we lived.

"You need to talk to your mom. I'm sure she's ready for them to come home. Tell her that they miss her," Liz said.

She's still in denial, I thought, *I've already accepted this and she is still in denial*. Not only had I accepted the situation, but I also knew it was best for them.

I went and talked to my mom anyway. Just to make sure she hadn't changed her mind. Not only had she not changed her mind, but she also told me she would come visit them and give us some money to help with them.

"I just don't understand," Liz said when I explained to her what my mom told me. "Why would you give your kids to someone else when you are able to take care of them? This isn't fair!"

"I tried to tell you Liz, I tried to tell you she was serious about this! I tried to tell you she wasn't going to change her mind!" I was not sugarcoating it anymore.

"So that's it?" Liz continued. "We get to figure this out now? What about us? What about Nate? How can we even afford to take care of everyone?"

"She said she'll give us some money every month to help," I said. Liz just shook her head. It was finally sinking in. It was finally sinking in that we now had three kids and two of them didn't want to be with us. She was very upset. This wasn't a responsibility she envisioned taking on.

MY BROTHER'S KEEPER: FAMILY OF FIVE

I decided it would probably be best to give her some space. Just let her calm down. She'll feel better about it in the morning. It would be Sunday and we would be headed to church. That's what she needed. She had rededicated her heart to the Lord last year and just like me, was trying to live a better life - one pleasing to Him.

"Good Morning," I said to Liz, trying to be optimistic. "I'm going to get the kids up. You want to start getting ready for church?" I asked.

"I'm not going," she stated.

"What are you talking about? It's Sunday! We always go to church on Sunday!"

"Well, I don't feel like it today. I'm not going!"

"So you're just going to stay here and keep being mad at everyone because you don't like what's going on? We need to take the kids to church," I said.

"Then take them," she said flatly and rolled back over in the bed. I couldn't believe it. When we started dating, Liz was the one who told me if we were going to be together, that I had to go to church with her. Now, when our family needs to go to church together, she refuses. So the kids and I went to church and Liz stayed home.

I don't know what all God and Liz hashed out while we were gone, but by the time we got home she told me she regretted not going to church with us. She apologized for being so upset with me. She admitted that she was ready for us to start a family of our own, but now she knew that wasn't going to happen anytime soon. This had really upset her.

Also, like me, it concerned her that we hadn't even been married a year and we were still trying to figure out how to be a family with Nate. As it was, we each had our own issues and now we were dealing with Cris and Johana's issues too. She didn't know how the new living situation would affect Nate. Johana and Cris didn't come from a Christian home. They cussed and lied and

NEVER ALONE

Liz was concerned about the negative influence on Nate.

Sometime, somehow in those next few days and weeks God began to show Liz that Cris and Johana were better off with us. Her heart began to change and soften. She began to want what was best for them, even if it cost her a season of her life. Over the next several months Liz, Johana, Cris, Nate and myself molded into this *Family of Five*.

Liz was very involved with the kids schooling, making sure their grades were on track as both of them were behind in school when they came to live with us. We made it a priority to stay active in church. By summertime, Cris and Johana even liked going to church.

Liz and I continued to grow in our relationship with the Lord. We both knew that if we were going to make it we had to have God's help. I was 19-years-old and Liz was 24. We didn't know the first thing about raising three kids, let alone ones who were 14, 8 and 6-years-old. We needed God! We couldn't do this on our own!

CHAPTER 7

MY BROTHER'S KEEPER

Part 2: Safe Keeping

"God is our refuge and strength, an ever-present help in trouble."

Psalm 46:1 (NIV)

NEVER ALONE

It was a Friday morning in early November 2003. I was leaving for a weekend trip to Tennessee for my first men's retreat with my church. In some ways I felt bad leaving Liz and the kids home alone, but I really needed this time away. I needed to grow closer to God and that was what the weekend was all about. Liz assured me everything would be okay.

I probably hadn't gotten past the state line when things started to turn upside down at home. Liz went to work as normal and Johana, Cris and Nate were in school. Liz had been at work less than two hours when she received a call from the boy's school telling her that their grandpa was there to pick them up.

"Mrs. Canales, Nathaniel and Cristian's grandpa is here to pick them up. Do you know about this?"

"I'm sorry, what?" Liz asked, trying to remember if her dad had asked to get the boys and take them somewhere. *Why would he be getting them from school and not even tell me anything?* she thought to herself. "I don't know anything about this. Are you sure he's there for my kids? What does he look like?"

"He's short...he doesn't speak very good English. He just keeps asking for Cristian and Nathaniel."

Liz's heart sank and she began to feel sick at her stomach. She realized who it was. It wasn't her dad. Her dad was tall and spoke English. "Please," she said sternly "do not let my boys see him! That is my father in law. He has been out of the country over two years and we had no clue he was back or how he has found the kids. Please do not let him see them! If he takes them I won't know how to find them! I'm leaving work to come get the boys now!" Liz told the school secretary.

"We'll take care of them," the secretary said before hanging up the phone.

Liz left work immediately trying to get to the boy's school as fast as she could. She wasn't sure what to expect. No one had even heard from my dad in a year and everything here was different than when he had left 2 years ago. I was married now. Cris and Johana lived with me and my mom lived in a different place with a roommate. Things were actually better. No one was dealing with his abuse – no one here at least. Since he'd been gone we had learned a few details about how he had been controlling and abusive to my sisters.

Liz wasn't sure how she was going to deal with my dad. She wasn't sure how she was going to explain to him that he needed to wait for a few days to talk to me before seeing the kids. He didn't speak a lot of English and she didn't speak a lot of Spanish. I was the only one who could handle him. My mom was scared of him and didn't want anything to do with him. Johana and Cris were scared of him too. It's hard to realize the depth of the abuse and dysfunction you are in until you are out of it and exposed to a different way of life. There is no perfect family – we all have our own things to work through. However, abuse is never normal – it is never okay!

Liz and I already had a few discussions about what we would do if he ever came back. I knew that eventually he would make his way back and find us, he always did. I also knew he would probably be mad that Johana and Cris were living with me now.

"Don't let him in the house unless I'm here," I told her. "Don't ever let him in if I'm not here." Liz didn't understand how dangerous he was. He was always on his best behavior around her and there was still so much about my past I hadn't even told her yet.

In the 20-minute drive to the boy's school Liz decided that she would not call to tell me what was going on. She didn't want to take a chance of me bailing out of the men's retreat, telling the group they would have to drop me off somewhere and go on without me. She was sure that God had something for me that weekend and she wasn't going to let anything stand in the way of

NEVER ALONE

me receiving it. She was also trying to call my mom and warn her that my dad was back, but she was having trouble getting ahold of her.

Liz was still trying to reach my mom as she pulled into the school parking lot, looking around to see if she could spot my dad. Walking into the school, she was scanning the area to see if he was still there.

"He left a few minutes ago," the secretary said. "We think he is headed to look for Cristian's sister because he was asking about the high school. We've already called them and asked security to hold him there."

"I need to get the boys and get to the high school," Liz said. "I have to get the kids some place where he can't find them until my husband gets home."

"We pulled the boys from class and had them eat lunch in the conference room," the lady said as she took Liz to the boys. Liz was relieved to see both of them sitting there eating lunch. As the boys went to get their belongings, Liz spoke to the office staff.

"Would you please watch us as we leave to make sure that the boys and I get in the van safely?" They agreed and they also called the high school to let them know she was on her way to get Johana.

Liz and the boys pulled into the high school parking lot. Again Liz was looking all around them, trying to spot my dad. She didn't know what he was driving so she wasn't sure if he was there or not. She parked as close as she could to the doors, grabbed both the boys by their arms and ran into the school, keeping an eye out for my dad. She wanted to see him before he could spot them. The high school office personnel were waiting. They pulled Liz and the boys into a room to speak to her privately.

"Mrs. Canales, security is holding your father-in-law in the other office. He thinks he is waiting for someone to get his daughter. He has another girl with him and she looks very frightened." Liz's heart sank. She knew that meant he had brought one of my sisters from Honduras with him. One of my sisters that I had no memory of – one of my sisters that I had only seen pictures of and spoken with on the phone a few times.

"I need to get Johana," Liz said. "I can't let the kids see him right now. I have to talk to my husband first. We had no idea he was back in the country let alone here in Indiana," she told the guidance counselor. "I believe it would be best for me to speak to my father-in-law without the kids and explain to him that I'm going to have Juan call him and they can go from there."

Cristian and Nate waited in the office as the guidance counselor took Liz to the other office where my dad and sister were waiting for someone to give them some answers.

"Hola," Liz said as they both got up to give her a hug. My dad began telling Liz that he didn't understand what was going on. He couldn't find my mom. He couldn't find us. He went to the kid's old schools and the office staff gave him the name of the schools they had transferred to. We then knew how he had found the boys.

"I want to see my kids," he told Liz. "Their sister is waiting to meet them."

"I know," Liz said, "I will have Juan call you." Liz was trying to not say anything that would let him know I was out of town. She could tell that my dad was getting aggravated and that my sister, who was with him, was scared. Liz apologized again and as she left the room, she asked the guidance counselor if she could speak to him privately.

"Can you hold them here until I leave with the kids? I don't know what he is driving and I don't want to take the chance of him following me home." The guidance counselor agreed, taking her to Johana's class.

Johana was in her drama group on stage in the middle of drama class. The guidance counselor pulled the teacher aside and told her they needed to speak with Johana. When Johana saw Liz she knew something wasn't right. Wondering if she was in trouble, Johana was trying to remember if she had done something wrong.

NEVER ALONE

"Your dad is back, Johana." Liz said. Johana immediately froze. She understood that Liz was there to get her and protect her. Liz hugged her and explained to her that she already had Cristian and Nate and that the school was going to hold my dad until the four of them could get off of school grounds. They were going to go somewhere where they would be safe until Liz knew what to do.

Liz still didn't know what my dad was driving and she wanted to make sure he wasn't following them, so she decided not to go home. Instead, she took the kids and went back to her work. He didn't know where she worked so they would be fine there, but she also knew that my dad did know where my mom worked. Liz kept trying to call and get a hold of my mom. The kids had been with us for almost a year now and she was still working second shift. Liz was afraid my dad would show up where my mom worked.

Johana was finally able to get through to my mom and tell her that my dad was back. She explained to my mom that he had already tried to go to the kid's schools and pick them up. They all agreed to meet my mom at her work and make sure that he didn't try to mess with her.

GOD HAD SHOWN ME SO MUCH ABOUT HIMSELF ... HE HEALED SOME AREAS IN MY HEART THAT I LAID BEFORE HIM.

As planned, Liz and the kids met my mom before her shift started. Mom was hugging the kids and telling them not to worry, when my dad walked up on them. He began asking my mom what was going on. He told her that they needed to talk. He told her that he was back and he brought her daughter. When my mom wouldn't talk to him, he became frustrated and started getting in her face, not letting her go around him. Finally, he convinced her not to go in to work but instead to go and talk with him somewhere else. Liz was afraid to leave my mom alone with him, so she suggested that they all go to a nearby McDonald's to sit down and talk. Liz knew I wouldn't be happy that she took the kids and went with them, but she was afraid of what would happen to my mom if they weren't there.

After that meeting, my mom ended up going back to our house to stay with Liz and the kids all weekend. Liz also ended up giving my dad money to stay in a motel until I could get home. She still didn't want me to know anything about what was going on while I was away. She knew I would need whatever strength God was giving me that weekend to get me through whatever was coming next in our lives.

Sunday evening I was on my way back home from the men's retreat. It was awesome! God had shown me so much about Himself and his love for me. He healed some areas in my heart that I laid before Him. I was ready to get home, be with my family and begin what felt like a fresh start in life. I called Liz to let her know about what time I would be home.

"I need to tell you something," she said. I could tell she was hesitating. I'm sure it was because she didn't know how I was going to react.

"What's going on?"

"I need to tell you before you get home. I don't want you to be surprised when you get here."

"What is it?" I asked. She began by telling me that my dad was back and then she shared everything that had happened over the weekend. I couldn't believe it. I felt like the air had been knocked out of me. Over the weekend I had reached a real turning point in my Christian walk and now this was waiting for me at home.

"He hasn't been staying at the house has he?" I asked her.

"No. I gave him money for a motel room, but he is here now waiting for you to get home. He doesn't understand why Johana and Cristian are living with us instead of their mom."

NEVER ALONE

"Well, did you tell him it was because she told us if we didn't take them that she would let them go to foster care?"

"No, Juan. I think he thinks we took them away from her," she said.

"Are you serious? He thinks we took them?" I was getting upset.

"You're going to have to explain to him what happened that night. I'm not sure why he thinks we took the kids but there's something else. He has one of your sisters with him. Yuli is here."

Wow! I couldn't believe what was going on. I would be home in a few hours and would be dealing with my mom and my dad, Johana and Cristian, and now my sister was there too.

Yuli was only 20 months younger than me. We were not raised together and I had no memories of her. Less than two years separated our births, yet our lives had been completely different. I had been raised here in the U.S. trying to handle whatever life threw at me and she had been raised in an orphanage in Honduras. I knew very little about her or what she had experienced in life and she knew very little about me and what I had experienced – other than the lies I was sure she had been told. I wondered if we had been raised together would we have been best friends?

I came home that evening to Liz, Nate, Johana, Cristian, my mom, my dad and my sister Yuli. My dad didn't understand why everything was different. He wanted to know how everything had happened. He also didn't have a place to stay since my mom lived with a roommate. Which also meant Yuli didn't have a place to stay. I had worked on forgiveness this past weekend, forgiveness towards both of my parents. I guess I thought to some degree I was being tested in this area. I agreed to let my dad and sister stay with us until he could get on his feet.

"You're going to have to get a real job," I told him. "This is only temporary. You have to get a place of your own." He agreed to go out the next day and start looking for a job.

MY BROTHER'S KEEPER: SAFE KEEPING

So much happened over the next few weeks. Liz and I had to go to work and the kids were in school during the day. That meant my dad and Yuli were left at my house alone. I found out several months later that during this time, my dad had gone into our bedroom and gone through our important papers. He took copies of birth certificates and social security numbers for Liz, Nate and I.

Also during the time he stayed at our house, he would have conversations with Johana and Cristian behind my back – saying things like he was going to get them back and that I shouldn't have taken them away from my mom. I also learned the reason he thought I had taken them away was because that is what he had been told. He didn't believe me when I tried to tell him the truth.

During the three to four weeks that I let him stay in our home, I noticed Johana and Cristian's attitudes becoming worse and worse. Johana was afraid that she was going to have to go back to live with him when he moved out. He had been talking to my mom. They decided they were going to get back together again and take the kids back to live with them. He had been telling this to Cris and Johana.

I told him before I let him stay with us that this was my house and he couldn't act like it was his. He had been gone from our lives for over two years. Liz and I had been taking care of the kids for the last year. I told him that he needed to let me handle them. It all blew up one night over an issue with the kids.

He had gotten on to one of them over something and he didn't like it when I told the kids to go ahead and go upstairs. When he tried to argue and tell me that they needed to stay downstairs, I said no. He became very upset and acted like who was I to tell him anything?

The man who had abused my mom, my sister and me was right here in my living room ready to go toe to toe with me. This man, who, when something triggered him, became like a possessed man with super human strength was right in front of me. I knew that it didn't matter to him who you were, when the trigger went off, he would use whatever he could to beat you.

Memories of the last time he beat me flooded my mind. That was just two and half years ago. Fast forward to this blow-up point. I was married with three kids, living in my own home, taking care of my responsibilities and my dad's, and he's ready to go at it with me.

"If you don't like it, you'll have to leave," I told him. "I'm the one who makes the rules here."

"So you'd put your own father out on the street? I thought you were a Christian!" he said.

"It's your choice if you go, but you can't stay here and think you are in charge. Get your own place if you want to be in charge. This is my place," I told him.

"I can't believe you would kick me out knowing I have nowhere to go," he yelled.

"Okay, I guess you've made your decision then!" I said. He began causing a big scene, yelling up the stairs to Johana and Cris, telling them that I was kicking him out. At this point I told him he needed to go or I would call the cops. I told Yuli that if she wanted to stay I would do what I could to help her, but he insisted she go outside and talk to him and she went. A few minutes passed. I looked outside and they were gone.

Well, that was done. It could have ended a lot worse than it did. The truth is, it was far from over. As the next few months played out Liz and I would be given *Our Assignment*.

CHAPTER

8

OUR ASSIGNMENT

"May He equip you with all you need for doing His will. May He produce in you, through the power of Jesus Christ, every good thing that is pleasing to Him. All glory to him forever and ever! Amen."

Hebrews 13:21 (NLT)

NEVER ALONE

It was a Sunday night and we had just gotten home from church. Christmas was only three days away. Things were starting to get back to normal at our house since my dad had been gone for a few weeks. The kids were excited to open all their presents under the tree. Cris and Johana had been living with Liz, Nate and I for a year now. This would be our second Christmas together as a family of five.

We were all sitting in the living room when we heard a knock at the door. We weren't expecting anyone and it was too late for someone to be randomly knocking on the door. I answered it. In front of me stood a sheriff with my mom. He asked if they could come in. He began explaining to me that he had been asked to come and get the kids and give them back to my mom and dad. I asked him if he realized the kids had been living with me for a year now. Of course he did not.

"Do you have any paperwork showing you are the legal guardians of the children?" he asked.

"She signed third party guardianship over to me last year," I explained to him.

"Has a court appointed you their guardian?" he asked.

"No, she gave them to me a year ago and we haven't had any issues until my dad came back to town. That is why all of this is happening now. She doesn't really want them. She's doing this because my dad told her to and she is afraid of him."

I had a feeling my parents were going to try something. Since he had been back in town, my dad had been making comments to the kids about taking them back and my mom wasn't really talking to me anymore. I just didn't expect this three days before Christmas.

What my parents didn't know was that the kids had been telling us everything. He told them they wouldn't be allowed to live with Liz and I any longer. He told them that it didn't matter what they wanted, he was back and

OUR ASSIGNMENT

he would do whatever he needed to do to get them back. Liz and I took these conversations very seriously. I knew my dad would do whatever he wanted to have his way. The kids didn't want to go back and live with my parents. They were scared of my dad and knew my mom couldn't protect them from him. They needed security and stability and somehow over the last year God had helped Liz and I to provide that for them.

When the kids started telling us about my dad's comments, Liz began researching what rights, if any, we had in order to keep them in our home. Basically, the only thing we could do was hire an attorney and pursue Permanent Guardianship. How were we going to afford an attorney? We didn't have the means to do that. So we needed to work something out with my parents without going to court. We decided to wait and see if my dad would calm down. Even though I knew he would eventually make his move, I needed to wait and let him do just that.

So in that moment, with the sheriff and my mom standing at my door, Liz's research proved to be critical. She found out that if the kids did not want to go back with my mom, all they had to do was tell the officer and he couldn't make them go with her. There was one risk. If my mom wouldn't allow them to stay with me, and the kids refused to go with her, they would be taken to foster care until we could go before a judge.

I had suspected that my parents would show up at the kid's school with a police officer to try and take them back. So, we had been telling the kids that if my parents came to get them, all they had to do was tell the police officer that they didn't want to go and the officer wouldn't make them. I was a little surprised when my mom and the officer actually came to my house. The officer told the kids that their mom was there to get them and they needed to go with her. Johana told him she wasn't going – that this is where she had lived for the last year and she wasn't moving again. She didn't want to live with her parents again. The officer didn't seem to be expecting that the kids would refuse to go.

NEVER ALONE

At this point things got a little chaotic. My mom had brought a friend to translate for her. She didn't understand why the sheriff wasn't making Cris and Johana leave. Mom is telling the kids to come on and they are crying and telling her no. The sheriff is trying to explain to her through her translator that if the kids are refusing to go, he couldn't make them. He also told her that if she didn't allow them to stay with us, he would have to take the kids to foster care that night and they would stay there until a judge could hear our case. He told her we probably wouldn't be able to get before a judge until after Christmas. That meant that the kids would spend Christmas in foster care.

I could tell my mom wasn't expecting that. She thought that the police officer would handle this and that she would be taking Johana and Cris back that night. She was so mad, but thank God she went ahead and let the kids stay with us and didn't make them go to foster care that night. The whole ordeal lasted probably an hour.

I remember closing the front door and locking it. We were all shook up. There was only one thing we could do. The five of us got in a circle, held hands and began to pray. We thanked God that He had kept us together for another night and we asked Him to help us get through whatever lay ahead. My parents made the first move. Now, Liz and I had to move forward and do what we could to protect Johana and Cris.

We had been seeking advice from a family law attorney. The next morning, Liz called him and told him about what happened the night before. She asked him what we could do to keep the kids safe. We were afraid that once Christmas was over my parents would come back with a sheriff except this time, when the kids refused to go, my parents would have the officer take them to foster care.

The attorney immediately began making phone calls trying to get an Emergency Hearing to grant us Temporary Emergency Guardianship of the kids. A day or two later he called to tell us we had an Emergency Hearing with the judge just a few days after Christmas. We couldn't believe it! We had been granted an Emergency Hearing in the judge's chambers during the holidays! Our attorney couldn't believe it either.

So much had happened in just a short amount of time but so much more was on the horizon. It was stressful. It was hard, but there was something unfolding that brought so much joy to me. On Christmas Eve 2003, Liz told me we were having a baby! I was raising three kids already and now God was trusting us with another one. I was so happy! In the midst of all the craziness with my parents, this child in my wife's belly brought so much happiness and hope to our family!

The next day was Christmas. I had told my mom the night that she came to take Johana and Cris that she and my dad could come see the kids for a few hours Christmas morning. I look back now and see how God's grace compelled me do to that. They had been so mean and hateful towards Liz and I when we hadn't asked to be put in this situation to begin with. We understood that if we were going to really do what was best for the kids, it would cost Liz and I too. Things were awkward that Christmas morning, but I know I did the right thing. It wasn't easy but it was right.

A few days after Christmas, Liz, the kids and I went with our attorney to the judge's chambers for our Emergency Hearing. The judge listened to a little bit of the backstory – how the kids came to live with us and why they didn't want to go back to live with my parents. He asked both of the kids if they wanted to live with their parents and they both told him no. Within 30 minutes we had been granted Temporary Emergency Guardianship. The kids would remain in our care until we had an official Guardianship Hearing. My parents would not have the opportunity to try to take them, even with a sheriff, again. They would remain in our care until the judge said otherwise. This was a huge victory. Our attorney said he had never seen this happen before. This took a huge weight off our shoulders.

NEVER ALONE

Our attorney immediately began preparing for our next court date and the final Guardianship Hearing. Once my parents found out that we had been granted Emergency Temporary Guardianship without them even being present, they were very angry. They cussed me out over the phone and told me how I had broken the law. They told me that they would get Johana and Cris and I would regret it.

Our next hearing was only a month away. My parents were still very angry. Our attorney advised me to try talking with my mom to see if we could come to an agreement outside of court. He said our chances of keeping the kids didn't look good as both of my parents said they wanted the kids back, neither of them were drug addicts and there was no documented abuse with the authorities. I called my mom the night before our first hearing. It was my 20th birthday. I told her that she knew it wasn't best for the kids to come back and live with them. She knew what my dad would end up doing not only to them, but to her. She cussed me out and hung up. She wasn't going to work anything out.

The next day we went to our first hearing. It lasted two to three hours. It was horrible. Here I was, trying to take care of my brother and sister who would have been in foster care if I hadn't taken them in. All we were trying to do was provide a safe and stable home for them, which none of us ever had. Had my mom placed the kids in foster care over a year ago, she wouldn't have been allowed to get them and take them back whenever she wanted. And just because they were with me she shouldn't be allowed to just take them back either, especially if they didn't want to go and especially if my dad was in the picture. How was it fair that Johana and Cris should have to live life with my dad's abuse wondering where they would be living tomorrow or what school they would be going to?

These kids had made so much progress in the short year they had been with us. God had done such a work in them and I didn't want to see everything undone just because my parents were being selfish. At the end of

OUR ASSIGNMENT

the hearing the judge determined that the kids would continue to live with us until the final hearing in April, however, there was a new twist. He set up visitation between my parents and the kids – unsupervised visitation, which made us very nervous. Nervous that my dad would just take them and leave the country.

Dealing with my parents for visitation was difficult just because my dad wanted it to be. Luckily there was no overnight visitation, but it was planned for every other Sunday, which took the kids out of church. They weren't happy about it, but it was what the judge ordered. The judge advised that we all work together and be flexible for the benefit of the kids. My dad proved he wouldn't be flexible at all when it came to visitation.

Johana had a youth trip that happened to be on a visitation weekend. The teens were headed to Tennessee for a youth conference and Johana really wanted to go. She had never been on a trip like this before. Someone in the church even paid for her trip. From the looks of it and between all of the conversations with my parents, they weren't going to budge and switch weekends. They were probably hoping that I would send her anyway (which I wanted to) and be held in contempt of court, but I wasn't going to play that game. My parents unwillingness to switch weekends and allow Johana to go to the youth conference only proved what I had been telling the court all along. They weren't concerned about the best interest of the kids.

A few days before the youth group was to leave our attorney got involved. My parents weren't budging and he was trying to get the judge to order my parents to switch their weekend. The Friday morning that the youth group was leaving came and went. We hadn't heard from the court so we couldn't let Johana leave with the group. She was so upset. About mid-morning Liz got a call from the attorney. The judge signed-off on the request, allowing Johana to go on the trip after all. He wasn't happy that my parents weren't willing to be flexible, so they didn't even get to reschedule that visitation. They just had to wait until the next scheduled Sunday.

NEVER ALONE

Even though the youth group left earlier that morning and Johana would miss the first service of the conference, when we got off work we drove her down to Gatlinburg, TN to meet up with the youth group. She would have the rest of the weekend with them. If God had moved on the judge's heart to grant Johana permission to go, then God must have wanted her there and we were going to get her there. We literally dropped her off at the hotel with the youth group, turned around and headed home with the boys. We were so happy that she got to have that experience.

We never knew what to expect after the kids came back from visitation. Some days they were just as happy as could be. They would come back with lots of "stuff." I knew what was happening and I knew it wouldn't last. Other times they would come home and Johana in particular would be very upset.

Our hearing for Permanent Guardianship of Cristian and Johana was held on April 5, 2004. Liz and I made our way to the City County Building in Indianapolis where the hearing would be held. We met up with our attorney in the hall to discuss some last minute points in our case.

"I do not advise that we seek child support. If we do they will argue that this is your motive and not the well being of the children," he said.

"Okay," I responded. It made sense. We didn't want the judge to question our motives. God would provide for us.

Liz and I spent the morning being questioned, drilled and insulted by my parent's attorney. He definitely didn't hold anything back. He did everything in his power to cast doubt and to question our character, all the while minimizing the abuse I myself had endured from my father.

After lunch when the hearing reconvened, we got to sit and listen as a court appointed translator translated lie after lie that my parents told about Liz and I. We could do nothing but sit there and take it, blow after blow. We were physically and mentally drained. I hadn't asked to be put in this situation, but my brother and sister needed me. They needed me to take the hits so that they wouldn't have to. I don't know why, but after everything I had been through in my life I was still kind of surprised at how I was attacked in the courtroom that day. Now Liz, carrying our first child together, was being dragged through this too. I felt so bad about the day she had just gone through.

> # THEY NEEDED ME TO TAKE THE HITS SO THAT THEY WOULDN'T HAVE TO.

We were surprised that the judge didn't make a decision that day. He said it would take him a few weeks to make his decision. The visitation should go on as ordered until he reached a verdict. We left court that day feeling pretty beat up and hopeless, but knowing that we had done everything we could. It was in God's hands now.

The kids continued the court-ordered visitation so we purchased a cell phone for Johana. Liz and I wanted to make sure if there was an emergency she could contact us. We didn't put it past my dad to just take the kids and run.

"Put it away. Don't let them know you have it," I would tell her. One Sunday afternoon when Cris and Johana were with my parents Johana called me and told me to come get her. Something had happened. My dad had threatened her and was acting like he was going to hit her.

"Call the cops! They can get there faster than I can!" I told her. By the time I got to where my parents were living, the cops were already there. My dad wanted Johana to do something that she didn't want to do. When she didn't do it he threatened to hit her. He wanted to make her respect him. When I got there he was so nice to me. He tried to get me to take his side over Johana's. He tried using the same line he used the night I moved out of his house – that it was all because of a disrespectful teenager. It was all Johana's fault. Obviously the police couldn't do anything. He hadn't actually laid a hand on her.

There was something else going on too. I noticed some issues between my mom and dad. My mom was very upset. We had been through this before. I knew he was being abusive to her but I also knew that she didn't want to say anything to me because of the Guardianship case. I waited until I could get a few minutes to speak to her alone and I asked her if she was okay.

"Is he hitting you?" I asked. She didn't respond. I knew he was, but why not say anything? Why fight for these kids to live with him? He was beating her and he would beat them. It was so frustrating!

Before I left their house that afternoon I was in the bedroom with my parents when my dad actually told me he was going to kill my mom. This was not the first time he threatened to kill her, but it was the last time I was going to put up with it. I remember looking at my dad's face. It was evil. I looked him straight in the eye and told him that if he planned to kill her he would have to get through me first.

"I'm not backing down from you anymore!" I said.

On June 3, 2004, almost two months after our hearing for Permanent Guardianship, we received shocking news. The court had decided to appoint Liz and I co-guardians of Cris and Johana. Our six-month battle to keep my brother and sister in our home and away from abuse was decided. We would assume full responsibility for them. Our attorney was as surprised as we were.

"I just can't believe this! I've never seen this happen before!" he said. Liz and I both knew that God had given us Johana and Cristian. He had given us *Our Assignment*. We hadn't been granted their guardians by accident. It was actually by Divine appointment. It was now our responsibility to raise them in a safe, stable home. It was a big assignment, but if God appointed us He would also equip us.

OUR ASSIGNMENT

We were all on this journey together – living, loving and learning. Learning that we were not defined by what anyone said about us but God! We did not have to be a product of our environment. That the old saying "the apple doesn't fall far from the tree…" really was nothing more than an old saying! We could believe for more and believe to be more because of Jesus! We could be different than anything we had ever known because of Jesus!

I think my parents were just as shocked as we were that we had been given Guardianship of the kids. The court ruled that the visitation every other weekend should continue and that we should let my parents see the kids as much as possible. However, after the judge handed out his decision, the kids might have seen my parents one or two more times before we quit hearing from them. No one heard from my mom for several weeks. When I would call to see what was going on even my dad said he didn't know where she was.

About six to eight months later, I found out that my mom had actually left my dad and filed for divorce about a month after Guardianship was decided. She finally admitted to me that he had been beating her and threatening to kill her, even while they were fighting us for the kids. My parents never reunited after this. My mom finally stayed away from him for good.

My dad ended up leaving the country again about a year and a half later. I haven't seen my dad in almost 11 years. I have spoken with him a handful of times over the phone. He mainly calls when he needs money. We sent him a little money a few times and then we stopped. He has given my address to people that he owed money to, telling them to come to my house and I would pay them. Needless to say, they aren't too happy when I tell them I'm not giving them any money to pay off his debts.

One day in particular only Liz and the kids were at home. A couple of guys showed up at our house looking for my dad. After Liz told them he didn't live there, they proceeded to tell her that we needed to give them back the money my dad had taken from them. She gave one of the guys my phone

NEVER ALONE

number to call me. He explained to me his family had given my dad money to bring a relative across the border. His family had received word from their relative that my dad had abandoned them and not brought them into the U.S. I was so angry at what he was doing to people and the danger that he was putting my family in.

"I didn't take your money, my dad did! I didn't have anything to do with this so leave my house now before the cops get there!" I told him in Spanish. After threatening me over the phone they eventually left. By this time Liz and the kids had gone back in the house and locked the door. From the upstairs window she watched them drive backwards down our street in a red car.

I've also received phone calls from people in Mexico trying to collect the money that my dad owes them. He would give them my phone number and tell them that his son would pay them.

The most disturbing call I received was from someone claiming to be my sister. She claimed that my dad had taken her, her sister and her mother from Honduras to Mexico. She said he was supposed to bring them to the U.S. but he actually ended up leaving them in Mexico. She went on to tell me that she and her sister were also my sisters. She also told me that my dad had been abusive to them – even as far as rape. It made me sick. She didn't ask me for any money. She didn't want anything from me, but she wanted to be sure I knew that I had two more sisters and that I understood what my dad was capable of. I knew what he was capable of. There is no way I can prove that she was actually my sister, but it was interesting. She knew a lot about our family and my dad's family from Honduras. I never heard from her again.

As for *Our Assignment*, Liz and I learned a great deal about ourselves and God during the time we had Cris and Johana. We didn't know how to do what He had called us to do, other than letting Him show us and He did just that. One day at a time. We weren't perfect and we have made plenty of mistakes, but God remained faithful! We truly wanted what was best for Johana and Cris.

OUR ASSIGNMENT

Johana lived with us for four years. She graduated from high school and was the first person in my family to graduate high school in the United States. Liz and I were so proud of her! She moved out and eventually got married. She has been married seven years now. They have a son and another baby on the way. They are doing great!

Cristian lived with us for 10 years. He graduated from high school and has been married now for three years. They also have a baby on the way!

I am very proud of both Johana and Cristian. They both have their own relationship with Jesus. They are hard workers and continue to not let the environment of our past place limitations on them. God has given them wonderful spouses to continue His plan in each of their lives! Now, I am transitioning out of the father role and into the brother role. Sometimes that's hard, even for Liz. We invested everything we had in them and they hold an important place in our hearts.

Looking back, it wasn't what we planned and it was much harder than we expected, but seeing the fruit of *Our Assignment* has made every second worth it! God's ways are much higher than ours and so is His purpose for our lives! Liz and I are thankful that God allowed us to be such a big part of His plan for Cris and Johana's lives.

Some assignments God gives us don't require a lot of time. Some do. Some don't require a lot of effort and others require everything you've got. One thing I know, if you trust Him and follow Him, He will give you the grace to do it. No matter how unqualified you think you are, He is greater in you!

CHAPTER

9

DEAD MAN WALKING

"You intended to harm me, but God intended it for good to accomplish what is now being done, the saving of many lives"

Genesis 50:20 (NIV)

NEVER ALONE

There are things in life that we may never get answers to. At some point we have to make peace with that. We have to continue moving forward.

In the summer of 2007 my mom came over to my house to visit. What I didn't realize was that she was bringing me life-changing information. That visit would leave me wondering many things. Some of those things I may never get answers to.

It was a beautiful, sunny Saturday afternoon when I got home from work. Like every day, my wife and kids were waiting for me. My mom was waiting as well. Sometimes she would stop by to visit my kids. While I was taking a moment to love on my wife and kids it seemed my mom couldn't wait to hand me a piece of paper. It was an official looking form in Spanish. I began to read it, wondering, *Is this a joke? This can't be real. I've been through some pretty messed up things in my life but this is crazy!*

I had to sit down. I looked down at the paper in disbelief. I was holding in my hands my own death certificate. According to Honduran authorities I have been dead since I was 4-years-old.

My mom began explaining to me that she had been trying to get copies of mine and my sister's birth certificates for us. When she requested mine she was told that they could not send her a birth certificate. Instead they would send my death certificate. I kept looking at this piece of paper to make sure it really had my name on it. This had to be a mistake.

"Are you serious?" I asked her. "Are you kidding me? Why did you do this? Why didn't you tell me about this?" My anger grew with each question. She said that my dad must have reported my death. She had no idea he had done it.

Questions were swarming in my head and as usual, I knew I wouldn't get many answers. When it came to my family, the questions always outnumbered the answers, but this was about me! This affected me! This was done to me! Why? My dad was nowhere to be found. I didn't know how to contact him and I never knew when he would try to contact me. Once again, more questions than answers.

What made this all so hard for me to grasp was that I was a father now. How can a parent disconnect from their child in such a way as to report him dead? How do you speak death to your child like that? What kind of benefit could there possibly be to doing such a thing? I couldn't connect with that on any level, emotionally or otherwise. I could tell my wife was angry and had as many questions as I did, but I had to get out of there. I had to be by myself before I exploded.

After a few moments of trying to collect my thoughts, I called my pastor and told him I needed to talk. He invited me to come to his house. As we sat on his back patio I began sharing with him the absurdity that had just been dropped on me. It was actually comforting to hear that he found this just as ridiculous as I did. I wasn't over reacting or making it a big deal. It was a big deal! We talked for a while and he prayed with me.

THIS PIECE OF PAPER CAUGHT ME OFF GUARD AND SURPRISED ME BUT IT DID NOT SURPRISE GOD.

By the time I got home my mom was gone. Liz and I tried to make more sense out of it but we couldn't. We couldn't make sense as to why on July 28, 1988 at 11 a.m. my dad reported that I had died of a stomach infection in Tegucigalpa, Honduras. It also didn't make sense that on the same day he was given permission to bury me in the Municipal Cemetery in San Pedro Sula Cortes, Honduras almost four hours away from where I allegedly died.

Looking back now, here is what does make sense. The God whom I had served for only a short time at that point, had His hand over my life from the beginning. It doesn't matter what people, even your own family, speak over you or even if an entire country believes you're dead. You see, death has been spoken over me from the time I was in my mother's womb. God says, "The thief comes only to steal and kill and destroy; I have come that they may have life, and have it to the full," John 10:10. God, and God alone has spared my life!

This piece of paper caught me off guard and surprised me but it did not surprise God. Psalm 27:10 declares, "Though my father and mother forsake me, the Lord will receive me." This tells me that whatever the reason my dad did what he did, God had me in His hands all along. He still does! I can count on him!

About a year later, God began to show me His purpose regarding my death certificate as I sat before a United States Immigration Judge in Chicago, IL. I realized it didn't matter the purpose behind reporting my death in Honduras. The Lord allowed it because He had a purpose as well. Romans 8:28 says, "And we know that all things work together for good to them that love God, to them who are the called according to his purpose."

Jeremiah 29:11 says, "'For I know the plans I have for you,' declares the Lord. 'Plans to prosper you and not to harm you, plans to give you hope and a future.'" There were obviously two plans in motion in my life at an early age. God's plan that gave me hope and a future and the enemy's plan to kill and destroy me. If I had really died at 4, I would not have met my wife and gotten married. I would not have had kids, no seed line! I would not have been here to raise my younger sister and brother and there would be no generational impact! But God!!

I can only imagine the war going on in the spirit realm where Satan is trying to take my life but God says, "NO!" God says, "Juan will live and not die! Juan will have a seed line! Juan will break the curse over his bloodline! Juan will make a generational impact!" Want to know what God says about you? Replace my name with yours! That is God's will for all of us!

DEAD MAN WALKING

Several years later my dad called and I asked him why he reported my death. What was his purpose? Did he show a body? His response didn't surprise me – he said he didn't do it. "Documents are falsified all the time," he said. "I would never do that to you."

More recently I asked one of my sisters in Honduras to see if there was any more information she could get regarding my death. They gave her the same information my mom had already given me. If we wanted anything further we would need to come back with an attorney. I'll be praying about if, when and how to proceed with that.

At the end of the day, God's purpose and plan trumps any other person or reason falsifying my death. I'm not dead! I'm alive! I am so completely blessed and alive in Christ! By His grace and mercy, I am not only breaking generational curses, but I am making a generational impact!

WHERE YOU START DOES NOT DETERMINE WHERE YOU FINISH!

CHAPTER

10

THE FIGHT OF MY LIFE

Part 1: Denied

"We are hard pressed on every side, but not crushed; perplexed, but not in despair; persecuted, but not abandoned; struck down, but not destroyed."

2nd Corinthians 4:8-9 (NIV)

NEVER ALONE

Life is full of experiences – both good and bad. We have experiences based on our own actions and we have experiences created by the actions of others, which can also be good or bad. Either can make us or break us. Sometimes, we are left to put the pieces back together that we didn't have any part of breaking in the first place. The fragments were left because of someone else's actions.

Sometimes, we find ourselves in circumstances that we have to deal with, work through, even fight through because we know the outcome will have a lasting affect on the rest of our lives. And not only our lives, but those coming after us. It's like we've come to a fork in the road. Life will turn out one way if we choose this path or it will turn out totally different down that path. This choice doesn't affect only us. It affects EVERYONE connected to us! We find ourselves in *The Fight of Our Lives*!

It was a cloudy Indiana day in January 2006 when Liz called me, extremely upset. We were finally getting used to our new "normal" with Alex just being about 2-months-old. Liz had quit her job to stay home full-time with him because of his health issues. I was now the only provider for a household of seven. We were both under a lot of stress and what she was about to tell me was really the last thing we needed.

"Your application to Adjust Status was denied," she said. "What are we going to do? We can't renew your work permit. You can't apply to be a Permanent Resident."

"What are you talking about?" I asked, confused. "My Political Asylum should allow me to renew my work permit and adjust my status." My immigration status was confusing and had always loomed over us. My parents told us that I had been granted Political Asylum on my dad's petition, however we had never seen any paperwork showing it had been granted. I had always assumed that the paperwork was out there somewhere. We had moved so many times it could have gotten misplaced or possibly sent to a previous address.

My parents always insisted that Political Asylum had been granted. I'm not sure why they believed this. I don't know who told them that. Probably one of the many people they had hired to file petitions and find answers that they never received. Unfortunately, I watched them get taken advantage of numerous times.

My parents believed my dad had been granted asylum when he filed in November of 1997. I was included on that application. Immigration laws allowed me to apply to adjust status to Permanent Resident one year after asylum is approved. In April of 2000, my parents applied for me to adjust status to Permanent Resident based on Political Asylum being approved. In my mind, this was all done.

This is why I was confused when Liz called me that afternoon after receiving a letter in the mail from the U.S. Citizenship and Immigration Services. The letter stated that my I-485 Application to Register Permanent Residence or Adjust Status had been denied because we had not submitted the paperwork necessary to prove the Political Asylum had been granted. The letter also stated that this decision could not be repealed and the case was closed. This application had been pending for almost six years! As long as the status was pending I was allowed to work and have a temporary legal status. Now, that it had been denied we were facing a whole new set of issues.

Without a valid work permit I could not legally work or have a driver's license. Once my current documents expired – that was it. We had to figure out what was going on with my dad's Asylum and why my Asylum couldn't be found in their system.

We began researching reputable immigration attorneys, however a good immigration attorney also came at a cost. It was a cost we weren't sure how to cover but we had no choice. We had to get to the bottom of this. Before the end of the month we met with an immigration attorney and paid the retainer for them to begin work on my case. Step one was getting to the bottom of the Political Asylum.

The attorney reached out to the Asylum office in Los Angeles since that is where our initial paperwork was filed. No answers there. Without answers they had to move on to USCIS (United States Citizenship and Immigration Services.) Finally, after a few weeks we had some answers. Not the ones we wanted, but finally some real answers.

February 6, 2006 we sat in my attorney's office as they explained my father did apply for Political Asylum in November 1997. However, on January 13, 1998 it was denied. We also found out that he had been detained by immigration several times and was actually ordered deported in December of 1990. To make it even more complicated, at some point he was granted Withholding of Removal. Which means immigration wasn't actively looking to deport him, but he also did not have the right to apply for legal documents.

I had to start all over with immigration.

One of the most frustrating misconceptions that people have is that if you are married to a U.S. Citizen, you are fine, you are safe – you have nothing to worry about. That is not true! My attorney explained to us that since my parents brought me into the U.S. undocumented, the only way Liz could petition for me, based on our marriage, was for me to leave the country and wait for the U.S. to process my paperwork. There was no way of knowing how long that could take. It could take six months, one year, three years – no one could tell us. We would be at the mercy of the U.S. immigration process.

In addition to the thousands of dollars it would cost to navigate the immigration system, our family would also be separated. Liz would be left here by herself to care for five kids. Remember, she had quit her job a few months back to care for Alex. The attorney went over strategies with us including an option called "Cancellation of Removal". But before I could

THE FIGHT OF MY LIFE: DENIED

apply for Cancellation of Removal, I first had to be in Removal Proceedings, which meant deportation! The "D" word. The worst thing that could happen was deportation!

It was all overwhelming! There was so much to think about – and trust me, we thought about it – a lot. Our situation wasn't going to improve until we dealt with it. Thankfully, we had a few months to think and consider our options.

In April, our attorney called and advised us to put everything on hold. There was potential for upcoming legislation changes in Congress. If passed, this legislation could change my whole case for the better. After several months of waiting, nothing came out of the proposed legislation. We were back to square one with Cancellation of Removal being my only option. We were back to the "D" word.

> **WE HAD A CHOICE. WE COULD EITHER TRUST IN GOD AND FIGHT FOR OUR FAMILY OR LIVE WITH MY IMMIGRATION ISSUE...**

The summer of 2007, we found ourselves at a fork in the road. For the first time since before we were married I found myself without a job. Now, with my work permit expired we had to deal with my immigration status – immediately. We had to deal with this situation that neither of us had created.

Since I was so young when I came to the U.S. with my parents, I didn't understand all the legal issues I would have later in life. Liz had no understanding of my immigration status when we got married. She only knew what I believed – that I was brought here as a child and was supposed to have had Political Asylum.

We had a choice. We could either trust in God and fight for our family or

NEVER ALONE

live with my immigration issue looming over us like a dark cloud. Believe me the enemy did use my immigration status against us. He used it to place fear, frustration, helplessness and hopelessness on both of us, but we knew we could not cower to those things the enemy tries to magnify!

What is a BIG problem to me is nothing for my God to handle!

Was the situation real? *Yes!*

Was it serious? *Yes!*

Did it affect innocent people like our children? *Yes!*

Did it seem overwhelming? *Yes!*

Was it a bigger battle than we knew how to fight? *Yes!*

We had to hold on to God's promises! We had to stand on God's promises! We had to believe God's promises! Liz would find encouraging scriptures and put them on our refrigerator like, Psalm 9:9-10, "The Lord is a refuge for the oppressed, a stronghold in times of trouble. Those who know your name trust in you, for you, Lord, have never forsaken those who seek you," and Jeremiah 17:7, "But blessed is the one who trusts in the Lord, whose confidence is in him." No one on this earth could fix this situation we found ourselves in. We had to rely on God!

At this point, I was illegally in the U.S. – again – only this time I wasn't a child. I was an adult. I was married with a wife and five kids who depended on me, not only to provide for them financially, but to be a father and to be there for them. I was very concerned and wanted to make our situation better, but I was unsure how to move forward. I was afraid of what the future held.

I loved my family more than anything. I finally had something I had longed for my entire life – my wife and kids. The thought of not being with them was too much. We had fought so hard to be together and stay together as a family and now it could all be ripped away from us.

I reached out to my attorney and told her I was ready to move forward

THE FIGHT OF MY LIFE: DENIED

with the Cancellation of Removal process. I was ready to move forward with placing myself in Deportation. I could have chosen otherwise. I could have chosen to try and live our lives as normal as possible. As long as I didn't have any
run-ins with the law, they would essentially ignore that I was here – but we knew we would always be looking over our shoulder waiting for me to get caught. Yes, our family would be together and we wouldn't be taking on an expensive immigration battle that we had no idea how we would pay for, but we would continue to live in fear.

I wasn't going to allow the enemy of my soul and the enemy of my future to keep a hold of me with fear. He would not be allowed to have power over me or my wife! I was going to turn myself into immigration and say, "Here I am. Arrest me, place me in deportation!"

If I was approved for Cancellation of Removal I would be granted Permanent Residency the same day. If not, I would be ordered "Removed" from the United States. I would have to volunteer to leave the U.S. within 30 days of the judge's decision or else a 10-year ban would be invoked on me, which means that I couldn't even petition to enter the United States again for 10 years.

It was an all or nothing kind of fork in the road. This situation was something we didn't get ourselves into and it was something we couldn't get ourselves out of. This was something we had to give to God 100 percent; not 50 percent, not 80 percent, not even 99 percent but, 100 percent.

Liz and I decided that we didn't want to live our lives constantly looking over our shoulder waiting for me to be detected but hoping I wouldn't be. We didn't want to live our lives with this shadow hanging over us, wondering if and when our family would be separated. So we decided to confront what the enemy was using against us to torment our minds and hearts and to compromise our family and look it straight in the eye. We decided that I

NEVER ALONE

would turn myself into ICE (Immigration and Customs Enforcement). It was all or nothing.

We were starting a battle that would either end with my Permanent Residency in the U.S. or my being ordered to leave the United States of America, the country I had lived in for 18 years.

In the midst of all of this, Liz made a decision in her own heart, one that was difficult for her and her side of the family. She decided that if I was not allowed to stay in the United States, she and the kids would go to Honduras with me. I would never have put her in that situation. Life in Honduras would be completely different than anything she had ever experienced. Despite everything, she planned to sacrifice leaving her family and lifestyle in the U.S. She was adamant that God's plan for us would be done! Whether His plan kept us in the U.S. or placed us in Honduras, the most important thing was that our family stayed together!

"We either serve God here or serve God there! Either way we serve Him together," she would say.

We made these decisions completely by faith. Not just the faith that God would work this situation out the way we wanted, but faith that ultimately God's will would be done in our lives!

CHAPTER
11

THE FIGHT OF MY LIFE

Part 2 - Mistaken Identity

"So do not fear, for I am with you; do not be dismayed, for I am your God. I will strengthen you and help you; I will uphold you with my righteous right hand."

Isaiah 41:10 (NIV)

NEVER ALONE

My attorney began preparing the paperwork necessary for me to turn myself in. She began contacting immigration officials in Indianapolis to explain my unusual situation. We needed to reach an agreement with them. Once I turned myself in and after I was processed, would immigration release me to go back home? Would they allow me to continue to work and live with my family until I could go before a judge? I had to be assured that once I was processed I could go back home to my family.

In September of 2007, my attorney was advised by a supervisory special agent to write a letter to the resident agent in charge of Homeland Security in Indianapolis. This letter should include parts of my history explaining why I would be turning myself in, our intent to apply for Cancellation of Removal once in removal proceedings, and why I qualified to do so. We were assured that once I turned myself in and was processed (as long as everything verified properly) I would be released. The supervisory special agent would even meet us downtown to sign off on the paperwork. As a part of this process, a warrant for arrest of alien was issued and a date was set for me to turn myself in. There was no turning back now.

On Thursday October 11, 2007 at 12:00 p.m. I turned myself in to Immigration Customs and Enforcement in Indianapolis. My wife and attorney were with me. After checking in, we sat down and waited for the agent to call my attorney and me back to his office. Liz would not be allowed to go with me. My attorney assured us that everything should go as planned. They would take me back, ask me some questions, take my fingerprints, have me sign some paperwork and send me on my way. Once my name was called, it shouldn't take any longer than an hour or so.

I felt like a criminal as I sat in that immigration lobby. I was there to turn myself in for a crime committed by my parents when I was 6-years-old. Coming to the U.S. was a crime – even though I had no control over it – a crime that I now I had to pay for. I hated this! I had never been arrested. Now

THE FIGHT OF MY LIFE: MISTAKEN IDENTITY

I'm sitting next to my wife waiting to be arrested because my life can't move forward until this happens! I sat there with knots in my stomach, afraid that the ICE officials wouldn't keep their word and just deport me that day. I was afraid Liz would have to go home by herself and the promise I made to my kids that I would be back home in a little bit, would be broken. If this process didn't go as planned it could set our whole world in disarray.

> **HAD WE MADE THE RIGHT DECISION? WAS THIS REALLY THE BEST THING FOR OUR FAMILY? IT WAS TOO LATE TO CHANGE ANYTHING NOW.**

The enemy was attacking my mind with arrow after arrow. The battle going on in our heads and hearts was very real that day. Had we made the right decision? Was this really the best thing for our family? It was too late to change anything now. What was I going to do? Run out of an immigration lobby in downtown Indianapolis with special agents everywhere? I had to be still and know that HE IS GOD! I had to believe that no weapon formed against me shall prosper!

"Mr. Canales," the agent called.

Here we go, I thought. My attorney and I stood up. I looked at my wife as she tried to smile.

"Follow me please," the agent continued. We walked out of the main waiting room and down the hall toward another area where they processed and detained people just like me. However, many of them probably hadn't walked down the hall with the intent of turning themselves over to immigration.

We made some small talk – how are you doing – things like that. He told

NEVER ALONE

me his name. I'll call him "Agent C". He started the processing procedure, asking me basic information, like my name, address, date of birth, etc. He was kind to me. Not rude or harsh in any way. My attorney spoke with him regarding what had been arranged with his supervisors. So far everything was going exactly as she said it would. They took my fingerprints and sent my attorney and me back to the waiting room while they processed the rest of the paperwork. They would bring everything out once it was finished. Liz looked so relieved when she saw me come out.

Our attorney began talking us through what we could expect next. After maybe 10 minutes, Agent C came back to the lobby and in a very harsh and loud voice said, "Mr. Canales I'm going to need you to come with me."

I looked at my wife and attorney. Something was wrong. Something was very wrong. Agent C had been calm before but now he was a completely different person. My attorney nodded at me to go. As I walked past my wife towards Agent C I heard my attorney asking her, "Is there anything you guys haven't told me?"

"No! What's going on?" Liz asked. Her voice sounded like she was panicking.

As soon as Agent C had me around the corner from the lobby, he put me in handcuffs. He directed me down the hall we had walked through only moments ago making small talk. His tone was harsh like I was now his enemy. Ten minutes ago we had been friendly and now his demeanor had completely changed.

Back in the lobby my attorney was still probing Liz.

"Are you sure there isn't something you haven't told me?"

"No!" Liz replied.

"Well this isn't good and if they don't figure out whatever they are looking for they are not going to let him go," my attorney said.

THE FIGHT OF MY LIFE: MISTAKEN IDENTITY

Agent C directed me into a room then pointed his gun in my face.

"Take your shirt off!" he demanded.

Are you serious? I'm thinking. *This can't be happening!*

"Is there a problem?" I asked Agent C.

"Take your shirt off!" he said again, his gun still pointing at my face. This was crazy! I began unbuttoning my blue dress shirt. Then I pulled off my white tee. With his gun still on me, Agent C began to look at my chest, arms and back.

"Do you have any other tattoos?" he asked.

"No." I said.

"Have you had any tattoos removed?"

"No." I said. He examined the tattoo I had on my right shoulder.

"What do these initials stand for?" he asked, still very hostile towards me. I had gotten a tattoo a few years earlier. It was a cross with initials on each side of it. JC on one side and LC on the other.

"JC stands for Juan Canales. LC stands for Liz Canales" I said. He took my fingerprints again. He seemed to be calming down a bit so I asked him what was going on.

Agent C replied, "Your prints came back dirty. Your prints are in the FBI's system as a drug lord wanted out of California."

"Can I see the picture?" I asked.

"No, that's classified," he said. "There must be a glitch in the system. It's not you. You can put your shirt back on. I'll be right back. I'm going to speak to your attorney."

As I'm getting dressed I'm thinking to myself, *yeah, that's okay. Put me in handcuffs, point a gun in my face, tell me to take my shirt off and that my fingerprints are coming back as a drug lord wanted out of California and then don't even show me who you think I am! Are you kidding me?* I couldn't make this stuff up.

The devil showed up that day trying to once again gain control of my future. God showed me first hand again what He meant in Isaiah 54:17 when He said, "'No weapon that is formed against you shall prosper, and every tongue that shall rise against you in judgment you shall show to be in the wrong. This is the heritage of the servants of the Lord: this is the righteousness or the vindication which they obtain from Me,' says the Lord." Wow! God and God alone brought swift answers and vindication to me that day! We were literally fighting hell.

After I got dressed and everything calmed down, I signed the Notice of Custody Determination, which meant that I had been released on my own recognizance. I was advised to carry this paperwork on my person at all times. I had to affirm that I would comply when I was ordered to appear before an immigration judge of the United States Department of Justice in Chicago. Once all of that was done, I was free to go. I couldn't wait to get out of there!

That *Mistaken Identity* could have cost me everything – BUT GOD! God was my ever-present help in time of trouble that day! The United States of America may not have known who I was but God did! The Immigration of Customs Enforcement may not have known who I was that day but, God did! My attorney and even my wife could have doubted who I said I was for a moment that day, but God knew who I was! I was His son!

CHAPTER 12

THE FIGHT OF MY LIFE

Part 3 - A Man Without A Country

"The Lord is my shepherd, I lack nothing. He makes me lie down in green pastures, he leads me beside quiet waters, he refreshes my soul. He guides me along the right paths for his name's sake. Even though I walk through the darkest valley, I will fear no evil, for you are with me; your rod and your staff, they comfort me. You prepare a table before me in the presence of my enemies. You anoint my head with oil; my cup overflows. Surely your goodness and love will follow me all the days of my life, and I will dwell in the house of the Lord forever."

Psalm 23:1-6 (NIV)

NEVER ALONE

My attorney told us it could take a year or more before my final court hearing to determine my Cancellation of Removal case. I would be required to make two or three appearances before the Immigration Court in Chicago prior to my Master Hearing. After only two weeks I received a letter from the U.S. Department of Justice Executive Office for Immigration Review. I had been ordered to appear before the Immigration Court in Chicago on Friday November 16, 2007 at 9 a.m. This was happening a little faster than I had anticipated.

Chicago was only a few hours away. The older boys were in school so Liz's parents watched the younger ones, Mateo and Alex, as we made our way to Chicago for my first court appearance. My attorney met us there. She said this hearing wouldn't take long at all. I would be brought forward and asked if I understood the charges against me. I would also be asked if I wanted an attorney appointed for my case or if I would provide my own. Even though it was a flat fee of $1500 each time my attorney went with me to Chicago, I would provide my own. I wasn't sure how I was going to afford my own attorney, but this was the *Fight of My Life* and I wasn't comfortable letting the court appoint one for me.

We were in and out in less than an hour. Before leaving my attorney stressed the importance of gathering the paperwork needed for evidence in my case. The amount of paperwork was massive. I had to have some sort of document with my name on it proving that I had been in the U.S. for the last 10 years. Not just a couple of documents per year, but one document for every three months for the last 10 years. That meant from January 1996 to 2006. For some people this really isn't a big deal. Yes, it's a lot of work but at least most people probably have the papers stored somewhere or know who to call to get copies.

My last 10 years took me back to when I was 12 years old. We had moved at least 15 times when I lived in Los Angeles. My parents didn't keep

THE FIGHT OF MY LIFE: A MAN WITHOUT A COUNTRY

paperwork like that. I didn't have mementos from my childhood, let alone a document proving that I had been in the U.S. every three months from the time I was 12 to the time we moved to Indianapolis when I was almost 16.

The only records we would be able to get were school records. Liz and I began to make a list of schools but I couldn't remember all of them. I contacted the last school I attended in L.A. when I started the 9th grade. I explained to them why I needed their help. They were able to pull my records from the Los Angeles Public School System and give me the names of seven schools they had record of. That helped so much! I knew who to call.

In addition to the 10-year history, we had to provide background checks from Indiana and California. We had to send copies of all tax returns, W-2's, pay stubs, all leases and mortgages, a list of monthly expenses, family photos, school and community records showing what our kids were a part of and how my deportation would negatively impact them.

We also needed to submit names, addresses and telephone numbers of individuals who were willing to submit statements to the judge on my behalf – for evidence of good moral character and how my deportation would cause extreme hardship to my wife and children. There was no need for us to get overwhelmed with what was required. We were going to give this everything we had, fight the best we could and expect God's will to be done.

I was required to go to Chicago to check in with the Immigration Court one more time before my Master Hearing. In the Spring of 2008 we received notice of the Master Hearing date. Liz had been working closely with our attorney to make sure every single piece of evidence we could pull together to strengthen our case was in place. Evidence for my case was to be in the judge's hands about two weeks prior to my court hearing. We met with my attorney to go over the petition and evidence that would be sent to the judge. She handed me a packet containing over 431 pages stating my eligibility for Cancellation of Removal under section 240A of the Immigration and Nationality Act. This packet contained letters from my wife, family, friends, my pastor, my kid's school teachers and coaches, even co-workers of my in-laws, all explaining what kind of person they knew me to be and why deporting me would be devastating to my family.

> **EVERYTHING WAS BEING LAID ON THE LINE. THE JUDGE WOULD REVIEW THE PAPERWORK AND... KNOW WHAT HE INTENDED TO DO WITH ME....**

Here it was. Everything was being laid on the line. The judge would review the paperwork and for the most part know what he intended to do with me before we ever stepped foot in the courtroom. Liz and I prayed and fasted. She put more scripture on the refrigerator, like 1 John 5:14-15, "This is the confidence we have in approaching God: that if we ask anything according to His will, He hears us. And if we know that He hears us – whatever we ask- we know that we have what we asked of Him."

Did we want to leave the U.S.? No! Were we praying that God would move on the heart of the judge to grant my Permanent Residency? Absolutely! We were specific with our prayers, but we also wanted God's perfect will for our lives and we prayed for that too! We came to this sacred place where we realized we needed His will above our will. We asked the Lord to give us the answer we wanted, but we were also prepared to submit to His will, even if it wasn't ours. We wanted His will to be done here on earth as it is in Heaven. So, no matter what this day would hold, we had God, we had each other and we were in agreement for His will to be done. Our hope was in God, not a man!

On Wednesday July 16, 2008 before the sun rose, Liz and I once again left

THE FIGHT OF MY LIFE: A MAN WITHOUT A COUNTRY

Mateo and Alex with her parents and headed to Chicago with family and friends for my Master Hearing before the United States Immigration Court. This time we took Cris and Nate with us. Some close friends rode with us and Johana and her fiancée followed us. Liz's brother and his family would meet us at the Immigration Court in Chicago. That three-hour drive went by way too fast.

On the drive Liz and I went over the questions my attorney had given us – our stomachs were in knots. Our attorney had also given a separate list of questions for everyone going with us that day so that they would be prepared to answer should the judge bring them in for questioning. I was so nervous that I would get a date wrong trying to repeat all of the kid's birth dates or I would get the timing of an event out of sequence and the judge would think I was lying.

I kept Israel Houghton's CD, *Alive in South Africa* on repeat. The song *I'm Still Standing* especially spoke to me. Specifically where he stops the song and talks about when he was a kid and he had one of those bags you could punch and it would come back up because it was "weighted on the bottom!" It had substance in it! Israel goes on to say, "He's hit me with his best shot, life has poured all it could on me and I've got a bounce back in my spirit!" I felt like he was talking right to me as I was driving on I-65 N towards Chicago.

I felt like he was telling me, "Yeah, this sucks. Your driving yourself to put you and your family at the mercy of the court and in 30 days you could have to leave life as you know it behind, but you are still standing! After everything the enemy has tried you are still here and standing, and not just here and standing but, you are blessed!" I don't know how many times I played that song, but by the time we got through morning rush hour to downtown Chicago, I knew I was blessed!

It was a bright, sunny, beautiful day in Chicago. The hustle and bustle of the morning rush hour had the parking garage I normally parked in already full. Thankfully I found a parking lot with open spaces not too far from the courthouse. We walked down the sidewalk and across the street with the sun beaming on our faces. This was the day we had left in God's hands. We were completely surrendered to His will.

Our family met and ate breakfast in the cafeteria of the court building. Liz and I didn't have much of an appetite. I ended up giving most of my food to Cris and Nate. When we were finished we took the elevator up to where our attorney was waiting for us. After we got off the elevator we turned a corner and went down a long narrow hall. Chairs lined the right side of the hall and doors with numbers were on the left. People were talking quietly, dressed professionally and preparing for whatever laid behind those doors for each of them. I remember it vividly.

There were a lot of people lining that hallway. Special agents patrolled the floor making sure there was order. We were right in the middle of it, all 15 of us. In addition to my attorney, Liz and myself, 12 more friends and family members were there to pray and testify on my behalf should they be called. There were countless others back home praying for us as well. That day had been clothed in prayer. My attorney and I found some chairs to sit in so we could go over some last minute details on my case. The rest of my group tried to find a chair or place on the wall to lean.

"Okay, it's time," said my attorney. "We can go in now." My stomach dropped as I hugged my wife. This was it.

> ***"Have I not commanded you? Be strong and courageous. Do not be afraid; do not be discouraged, for the LORD your God will be with you wherever you go."***
>
> **Joshua 1:9**

I was surprised when I walked into the courtroom. I wasn't expecting the room to be as big as it was considering the narrow hallway. I thought I would be going into a small room, but it was much larger. Large enough that everyone who came to support me that day could have comfortably fit, but they wouldn't let anyone else in. Not even Liz. No one except my attorney

THE FIGHT OF MY LIFE: A MAN WITHOUT A COUNTRY

could be in the courtroom while I was testifying. Inside there was a place directly at the front for my attorney and me to sit. As we waited for the judge to come in, my attorney and a prosecuting attorney for the United States Immigration Court made small talk. There was also a police officer and a court reporter in the room.

"All rise for the Honorable Judge B." We stood up as I finally came face to face with the person God would use to direct my future. My wife had prayed for him many times, asking that God's will would be done through him. This man, this judge for the United States Immigration Court had the power to do as he wished with me, but God had more power than him. Romans 13:1 says: "Let everyone be subject to the governing authorities, for there is no authority except that which God has established. The authorities that exist have been established by God." God placed Judge B in this courtroom at this exact time and place so that our lives would intersect and he would rule in my Cancellation of Removal proceedings.

"Mr. Canales please step forward," said the court reporter. I walked up to the witness stand. "Place your hand here and repeat after me." I placed my hand on what looked to be a Bible and swore to tell the truth so help me God!

"You may be seated," said Judge B. The court reporter began to address the judge.

"Your Honor, this is the case of the United States vs. Juan Canales..." *This just got serious*, I thought. I'd never thought of it that way before. It really did feel like the whole world was against me. The only country I knew, the one I claimed as mine was against me in this room.

I truly was *A Man Without A Country*. I no longer existed in Honduras since my dad reported my death. The U.S. wanted to deport me since I wasn't supposed to be here either. I lived in Honduras the first five years of my life, but I had lived in the U.S. for 18 years at this point. This was the only life I knew. My memories of Honduras had faded over the years and I didn't really

123

NEVER ALONE

know my family there.

My attorney began asking me the questions on the list she had prepared me for. Every once in a while, the judge would interrupt and ask me a question too. I don't know how long this actually took but it seemed like forever. Once my attorney was done it was the prosecuting attorney's turn. His questions came across in a way that made it seem deportation wasn't a big deal in my case. All I had to do was leave the country, have my wife petition for me and wait for the paperwork to process. *Yeah,* I thought to myself, *I guess it's not a big deal when you see this everyday and it's not your family being ripped apart.*

"It's not a big deal if you have to wait outside of the country" he said. "People do it everyday."

"My wife insists that she and the kids will come with me if I can't stay," I said.

"Well that's her choice, but it's not necessary for her and the kids to leave," he stated, matter-of-factly.

"She doesn't work outside of the home. She takes care of the kids. Who is going to provide for them?" I asked.

"The government will help them," he said.

"But, why should the government take care of my family when I can?" It was so frustrating! They didn't seem to care about anything other than the fact that I was brought into the United States illegally when I was 6 years old. Should we all be punished for it, including my U.S. citizen wife and kids?

At one point Judge B asked me if I were to be deported, which country would I want to go to. Inside I found this a little humorous, like they are sending me on some type of vacation.

"Puerto Rico, I guess," I replied.

"Why not Honduras?" he asked.

"Because I don't exist there. I'm dead in Honduras," I replied. We were beginning to get into something that none of us could really grasp and

THE FIGHT OF MY LIFE: A MAN WITHOUT A COUNTRY

understand. I had no answers to give them about my death certificate. My attorney showed it as evidence. I told them I had just found out about it last summer. The only fact I could add that wasn't actually on the death certificate was that my dad was the one who reported my death.

I had been on the witness stand for about an hour and a half maybe close to two hours when they decided to take a small break. I was not allowed to go out with my family. I had to sit next to my attorney. The process was

> **I COULD TELL SHE WAS NERVOUS. SHE WAS TRYING TO KEEP IT TOGETHER BUT HER VOICE QUIVERED.**

exhausting and it looked and felt like we were getting nowhere.

After the break they called Liz in to testify. I could tell she was nervous. She was trying to keep it together but her voice quivered. I hated that Liz had to go through this. My attorney began asking her the questions she had been told to prepare for. Questions like, where she was born? Where she had lived? Does she have family here? How and when did we meet? Did she work? How many kids do we have? Then my attorney asked Liz what she would do if I were to be removed from the country. Liz explained to the court that she and the kids would come with me. My attorney asked her why she would do that when she didn't have to.

"Because the most important thing is that our family stays together," Liz firmly said. My attorney had no further questions.

Now, it was time for the Government's Prosecuting Attorney to question her. Again, he came across as if it was easy for me to leave my family. It was no big deal for my family to be left alone.

"Mrs. Canales you are educated, you have a degree, you can get gainful employment," he said.

"Who is going to take care of my kids? We have four kids," she said.

"People do this all the time, Mrs. Canales. Kids go to daycare and family members help out," again implying it really wasn't a big deal.

"How is it not a big deal for my kids? Their father will be thousands of miles away and I'll be gone working. How is that not a big deal?" Liz asked.

"Mrs. Canales people do this everyday. It's only temporary."

"We wouldn't stay" she said, now crying. "We would go with him!"

"Mrs. Canales why would you do that? Why would you remove your kids from the U.S.?"

"Because it's more important that my family stay together. Because it's more important that my kids have their dad. Because it's more important that my husband not be abandoned by people who are supposed to love him! I will not abandon my husband!"

I think all of her emotions, fears and frustrations came out at that moment. She cried so hard that they asked her to calm down. It was obvious that what was important in her heart and mind didn't make sense to the court – or if it did, I sure couldn't tell.

They were finished questioning Liz. I hated so badly that she had to go through this, but I was so thankful that she was my wife. She was doing all that she could to stand by me. No matter what, we would be together.

They dismissed both of us from the courtroom at that time. We were informed that the court didn't need to hear from any other witnesses. The judge had read all of the letters that our friends and family sent. He decided he didn't need to hear anymore. They would call us back in once Judge B made his decision.

Liz and I rejoined our family and friends in the narrow hallway. We were exhausted. Emotionally and mentally drained. I hugged Liz as she cried. Our

THE FIGHT OF MY LIFE: A MAN WITHOUT A COUNTRY

family surrounded us, wondering what had transpired. It didn't look good. The prosecuting attorney was adamant that it wasn't a big deal for me to wait "however long" outside of the country. The law states that if you come into this country undocumented at any age, even 6 years old, you are accountable for that action. By the questions the judge interjected, it seemed that he saw it the same way.

It had been about two and a half to three hours since I had gone into the courtroom for my Master Hearing. We spent all morning fighting for me to have the right to continue my life in the United States. My attorney assured us that it was okay that it was taking so long. She leaned against the wall and then slid down and began going over the notes she had taken during questioning.

I remembered the song I listened to over and over on the way to Chicago. Right now, I felt like I had been punched and I was down. As we waited to be called back into the courtroom no one was really talking. Everyone was very serious and praying.

"Is Dad going to be deported?" I overheard Nate ask his mom.

"We don't know," she said. "If he is, we're going with him. Our family will stay together."

Cristian would be starting his freshman year and Nate would be starting the 6th grade. There was so much at stake for our entire family. This affected everyone!

Someone peeked their head out of the court room. "You may come back in now." My attorney stood up and motioned for Liz and I to follow her.

Here we go, I thought. It had been a little over nine months since I had turned myself into Immigration and Customs Enforcement in Indianapolis. This was the moment we had been anticipating. The moment we had left in God's hands. Whatever decision was made we would comply, move forward and accept as God's will.

I sat down next to my attorney and Liz sat on a long wooden, pew-like

NEVER ALONE

bench behind us. The court reporter asked us to stand again as Judge B entered the courtroom. Once we were seated the judge began to speak. I don't remember everything he said. The courtroom was quite but, the noise in my head was deafening.

He began by speaking about the fact that I was brought into this country illegally. Despite my being married to a U.S. Citizen, I should have to leave the country and wait for the proper paperwork to process until I was allowed to come back legally. My stomach dropped. There it was. Within 30 days I would be leaving my life in the U.S. behind. Then, he went on.

"Mr. Canales you have a unique situation that I have never encountered before. I do not understand why your father would report you dead to Honduran Authorities. I do not know what it would take in order for you to prove your identity to them. Since you have not been there for so long, I don't know how you prove to them that you are Juan Canales. I cannot be sure that they wouldn't put you in jail until they figured it out. I also cannot be sure you would make it back to the United States. It is the decision of this court that you be granted Permanent Residency of the United States effective immediately. Congratulations Mr. Canales!"

I looked at my attorney. She smiled and reached out to shake my hand. I heard my wife crying. *That's it*, I thought. *What the enemy had meant to harm me God had used for my good!* I no longer had to wonder what the purpose of the death certificate was. God had used it for my good! God had used it to turn the heart of a judge and grant me Permanent Residency! Now, it doesn't even matter why my dad reported my death. What tried to speak death over my life God used to turn the whole immigration case for my good! That punching bag that had been down in the hallway a few minutes ago was up and standing. The enemy had thrown every punch at me that he could, but there I was – still standing!!!

> *"What, then, shall we say in response to these things? If God is for us, who can be against us?"*
>
> **Romans 8:31**

CHAPTER 13

THE FIGHT OF MY LIFE

Part 4: Dual Citizenship

"So then you are no longer strangers and aliens, but you are fellow citizens with the saints and members of the household of God."

Ephesians 2:19 (ESV)

NEVER ALONE

After my hearing I signed some paperwork with my attorney and that was it! Within two weeks I received my green card in the mail. July 16, 2008 was the day I was granted Permanent Residency. The day God granted us a huge victory!

I can't even put into words the burden that had been lifted off of Liz and I. Never again did we have to wonder how this would play out. It was almost kind of weird that we didn't have to do anything else at all with immigration until I was eligible to file for my Citizenship. We were so thankful!

I held my Permanent Residency for five years before submitting my application for Naturalization. It was time to prepare for my Citizenship Test. I would need to know the answers to 100 questions about the United States and be able write a sentence in English. Even though I would only be asked 10 of those 100 questions at the test, I was still very nervous. My language barrier made tests very difficult for me. What if I couldn't do this?

When we would go over the 100 questions and answers, even Liz missed a lot. She realized she'd forgotten a lot of U.S. History she learned in school. Out of the 10 random questions I could be asked, I was not allowed to miss any more than three. If I did not pass I would have to reschedule and be given the test again. If I didn't pass the second time I would be required to pay the filing fee again and reapply for Naturalization.

In the Spring of 2014 I applied to be a Naturalized Citizen of the United States. I began studying right away. Within three months I was called to take my test. Liz and I went to the Immigration office in downtown Indianapolis where I had turned myself in a few years prior. I prayed that the Lord would help me to remember everything I had studied. I needed to remember the answers to all 100 questions.

I was called back to begin the test. The agent asked me some questions about my background and began the oral portion of the test. After answering

THE FIGHT OF MY LIFE: DUAL CITIZENSHIP

the first seven questions correctly he told me that I passed that part of the test. *Yes! Thank God!* Next, he gave me a sentence to write.

"The White House is in Washington D.C." I nervously wrote the sentence he spoke.

Writing is not my strong suite. Even after all these years, I still have difficulty. I still blend English and Spanish together when I have to write.

"Congratulations Mr. Canales! You passed!" he said after reading what I wrote. I watched him stamp PASSED in big red letters on my paperwork. He began to explain to me what would happen leading up to my Oath Ceremony. I couldn't believe it! I passed! God helped me to remember everything I needed to that day!

THE PROCESS WAS PART OF DEVELOPING US!

Walking back to the lobby, I tried my best to fix my face on sadness and disappointment. I was going to mess with Liz and make her think I didn't pass. I kept a straight face as I entered the waiting room shaking my head "no" as I approached her.

"I didn't pass," I said.

She immediately said, "Whatever! Quit playing! I know you passed!"

I smiled and hugged her! We had come so far from that day she received the letter that the Asylum petition had been denied. We had put our lives, family and future in God's hands. In everything we had gone through He never let us down, not even once! Yes, we still had to walk through it all and endure every arrow the enemy sent our way, but God never let us down! The process was part of developing us!

NEVER ALONE

It was a beautiful morning in Indianapolis on Thursday, July, 24 2014 as I drove my family downtown to watch me take the Citizenship Oath. We parked and made our way through the metal detectors and security. I was surprised to find so many people there. I would be taking my oath with several other people who had their own immigration story. I checked in and took my seat at the front of the courtroom while my family sat in the designated section towards the back.

There was so much excitement in the room. People were taking pictures and laughing. I sat there taking it all in. I was so thankful for what God had done. This is the last thing I will ever need to do for immigration, but this oath isn't really for immigration. It's for me! It's for my wife and kids and family.

As we closed the immigration chapter of our lives we had learned so much and had so much to be thankful for! I am so proud that my kids could watch me take my oath and become a citizen of the United States of America!

I am proud to be a citizen of the greatest nation in this world. Yes, our country has its issues, but there is no other place in the world like this country! Some people, like my wife and children, are born with rights as a U.S. Citizen. I had to fight for those rights and that's okay! I appreciate those rights and will never take them for granted!

According to Philippians 3:20 "But, our citizenship is in Heaven. And we eagerly await a Savior from there, the Lord Jesus Christ." For many years, and I didn't even know it, I was not a citizen of any nation, but once I gave my heart to Jesus I became a citizen of God! A son of God! I proudly hold my *Dual Citizenship*! I am proud to be a U.S. citizen and a citizen of God!

CHAPTER

14

THE REFINERY

"Behold, I have refined you, but not as silver. I have tested you in the furnace of affliction."

Isaiah 48:10 (NASB)

NEVER ALONE

In 2008, right after I was granted permanent residency, I started working in a refinery. God blessed me with this job to provide for my family. He has also used my job and what I learned there to grow my relationship with Him – to help me understand things in a way I never would have unless I'd seen the process first hand.

We all know that as long as we are alive on this earth, we are going to have to go through some difficult times. Some of these situations will be hard. Sometimes they will be a little easier. Some of these times will be unfair and even painful, maybe even excruciating. Some of these hard places we've gotten ourselves into. Some of them we get thrown into, by no fault of our own, but we all go through some hard times.

I have to admit there have been instances when I have asked God, "Why me? Don't you see how unfair this is?" Of course He sees, but He isn't looking at things from our perspective – fair or unfair, easy or hard. His word says that His ways are higher than ours! He is thinking of our eternal well-being. As my pastor says, "He's gotta do a work in you so He can do a work through you!"

That is what God has been doing in me. For the last nine years I've been working in the refinery, but I've also been working through God's refinery. He has been doing a work in me. Showing me more of Himself and how I need to better reflect Him. You may be thinking, *Wow it's taken you nine years? Why so long?*

As I've shared throughout this book, I've been through a lot and in my own opinion, much of it hasn't been fair. I'm sure many of you have been through things that you didn't feel were fair. The enemy wants us to put ourselves down. He wants us to believe the lies and to be mad at God, but how can I be mad at the One who has forgiven my sin and pulled me off of a very destructive path? To be honest we should never want Him to quit refining us, because as long as we live in this imperfect world we need Him to keep pulling the impurities out of us! We NEED to go through the refinery – our souls depend on it!

THE REFINERY

A refinery is a place where a substance is refined. In the spiritual we can compare that to life. In the natural there are many kinds of refineries. I have heard that refineries are like snowflakes. No two are the same. All refineries have the same purpose, which is the refining process. Wikipedia says the process of refining consists of "purifying an impure material." In refining, the final material is usually chemically identical to the original one only in the end, it is purer. Isn't it interesting that the beginning and ending material is identical chemically? The only difference is that after the refining process the material is purer than it was before.

> **WE NEED TO GO THROUGH THE REFINERY. OUR SOULS DEPEND ON IT!**

When we are going through a refining season in our lives our DNA and biology stays the same of course, but we come out purer – more Christ like – a better reflection of Him. Ephesians 2:10 says, "For we are God's handiwork, created in Christ Jesus to do good works, which God prepared in advance for us to do." Just like the purpose of refineries are all the same, we all share the same Creator. His fingerprints are on all of us. According to Genesis we are created in His image. We were also created to do good works. They may be different good works but they share the commonality of being good and bringing our Creator glory!

Psalm 139:13 says, "For you created my inmost being; you knit me together in my mother's womb." Jeremiah 1:5a says, "Before I formed you in the womb I knew you, before you were born I set you apart..." The words I want to focus on here are knit and formed. When you think of someone knitting, you envision them using their own hands in the process. They are personally invested, adding their own touches. Each piece is unique. No two are the same. Just like us. When I think of forming something I see hands like God's hands forming each of us individually. To think that He physically touched everything He created blows my mind. Maybe when we realize that we are not accidents, but we are each very carefully formed and touched by the Creator of the universe, maybe then we will believe that He is careful with His creations in the refining areas of life too. He is not out to harm us, but to equip and strengthen us for this life on earth and prepare us to be ready when we see Him face to face. Absolutely nothing in life's refinery is without purpose!

In my particular experience in working in a refinery I learned that there are several phases in the refining process. First, the material is placed on a conveyor belt and goes into a crusher. We could think of the conveyor belt as time and the crusher as life. Time stops for no one. It continues to push us through the crusher or life process. The crusher turns the material into a nasty, ugly, muddy substance. Sometimes the crusher leaves us feeling beat down and a mess. We've all felt the crushing blows of life. I have felt that way many times.

Next, this nasty, ugly, muddy substance goes to a sink float. This is an area filled with water where all of the heavy material sinks down to the bottom. The stuff that is dense and not heavily weighted, or the waste, rises to the top to be thrown away. In other words the good stuff goes to the bottom and the bad stuff floats to the top. The heavy material, or the good stuff that was on the bottom, gets dragged on a drag chain conveyor belt. The material gets pushed through a shaft, which is moved by a large screw. Then it gets dumped in a designated area to dry. We could compare this to a resting time. When it's dry enough a loader picks it up and mixes it with another material and drops it onto a steel conveyor belt. It now goes into a big circular room where heat is applied and a spinning motion occurs. Ever feel like things are spinning out of control? Of course, we all have.

Now, the material is ready for the furnace. Sometimes in life we feel like we've already been in the furnace when actually, we were just being prepared for it. The furnace is heated up and incinerates all the bad stuff. It's all burned away. What is interesting about this is that different metals melt at different temperatures. Depending on what material you're dealing with determines how high the furnace is set. What's left of the material being refined is now liquid.

Again the heavy, pure stuff falls to the bottom and the impurities float up to the top. The stuff at the top is the waste or slag. There is nothing of value in this waste at this point. In terms of the spiritual furnace, God is burning off of us those things that don't bring value to our lives. Those things that do not bring Him glory. The good stuff, the valued material is found on the bottom. The lower it is the better it is. This makes me think of humbleness and recognizing our need for God. Mathew 20:16 says, "So the last will be first, and the first will be last." This doesn't mean we put ourselves down. We simply put others before ourselves. It also makes me think of us on our knees in prayer crying out to God. That is the most valuable position we can be in – on our knees, humbled before Him, praying and talking to Him. God sees value in us praying to Him. He actually values that a lot!

The good stuff then goes into a kettle and is burned again with high temperatures and treated with other pure elements to make the original material purer. I find this interesting: even though it has already been determined which substance is of value because it sank to the bottom instead of floated to the top, it is still necessary for it to go through the burning process again. Also, the good stuff is not good enough by itself. It needs to be treated with other pure elements in order for it to take on its purest form. I think of my own life. Coming through different trials and experiencing difficult times, I have watched how God has changed the way I acted, reacted or handled things.

Galatians 5:22-23 says, "But the fruit of the Spirit is love, joy, peace, forbearance, kindness, goodness, faithfulness, gentleness and self-control." I see how God has grown me in those areas – and He still is. After going through all that I had from an early age and into my teenage years, I wasn't

NEVER ALONE

the kindest or gentlest or most loving person in the world – until I accepted Christ as my Savior! Once I did that, everything I had already been through and would go through was for a purpose! In the refining process the good stuff is pumped into a mold giving it a new shape and form so it can fulfill it's purpose. In the same way, I wanted to mold my life after Christ so that I could take on my new form and purpose.

Let's go back to earlier in the refining process, where I said that the bad stuff or waste had no value at that particular point. Actually, the bad stuff goes back – through another process – like a second chance. I can tell you that I'm so glad that God has given me chance after chance. He has never given up on me. He sees me with all the good qualities and the purpose He placed in me from the beginning. He's trying to bring them out in me! He's trying to bring them out in you!

The waste, or the bad stuff, goes back through another heating process, just to make sure there isn't still some good stuff left in it that can be refined and used. Guess what! Every single time the waste is put back into the furnace there is still good and pure stuff sinking to the bottom! Every time more of the good material is pulled out through the refining process! Every single time! What came out as waste in the first process gets put back through just in case there is something of value in it and every single time there is! You have to get this! What you feel is a waste, what others may have told you is wasted, God is saying, "Let Me get a hold of that. Let Me fix this. Let Me turn this around. Let Me make beauty out of your ashes!"

If my company didn't have this process in place – to put the waste back into the furnace, making sure that all the good stuff was pulled out – they would lose millions of dollars. That's how important this so-called waste is. Do you think there is a difference in the quality of the "good stuff" from either process? The second batch of good stuff is just as pure as the first. It is placed into molds and is good enough to be used for the same purpose. The only difference is it took the second batch a little longer to get there. The value of

THE REFINERY

the so-called waste from the initial process still had good enough qualities in it to be refined and to be considered as good and as pure as the first. This reminds me of how God is so loving and patient with us. Acts 10:34 tells us that God is no respecter of persons. He loves us! We can't make Him love us any less!

I want to go back and tell you about a part of this particular refining process that I hadn't mentioned yet. I spent several years and thousands upon thousands of hours doing this particular process. As the material is in the furnace, melting into a liquid form and moving through the kettle, it's important that someone have the job of raking this liquid material. At this point in the process, the material looks like lava. It was my job to keep the refined material running so it didn't get hardened and stop the flow. If the flow stops, the lava spills over into unsafe areas and is a mess to clean up. There was nothing glamorous about being the raker, but it was very important to keep the liquid material running and flowing smoothly in the right direction. This process couldn't be done with a machine. A human had to actually walk back and forth, keeping watch and raking the pure liquid material. In the spiritual, I think of rakers as pastors and spiritual mentors that God places in our lives to watch over us. I'm thankful for the men God has placed in my life to watch over my soul.

One thing I know first hand is that in the raking position you will get burned. At my job I wore protective gear in order to insulate me from the elements of the refinery. Even with all of that gear on, there would be times where the liquid would splash up in just the right way and burn me. Remember, I said this was like liquid lava. It hurt very badly every time! And you never get used to it. Basically it's like liquid fire shooting up your sleeve, down your boot or up the back of your shirt. You will walk away with burn marks if you are the raker. If you oversee this process you WILL be burned!

In the spiritual if God has entrusted you to watch over souls you WILL get burned! That is part of the territory, but be encouraged. It's actually

NEVER ALONE

worth it to get burned because your job is important. Valuable material is still being pulled through the process to its destiny and God is using you to keep it flowing. Be assured that God sees every burn mark on you, the visible ones and the invisible ones! The rakers – parents, coaches, pastors and spiritual mentors – are very important to the refining process.

There is so much more to this process that I could include, so many more correlations of what God has shown me through this refining process, but I hope you can now see how important being refined is to our spiritual growth. If everything always went our way would we ever really feel we had a need for God? Would we ever rely on Him wholly and completely? He wants us to rely on Him in the good and the bad. Just like He loves us in the good and the bad.

My wife asked me one day if I could see my reflection in the liquid lava as I was raking it. At first I told her no, but a few days later I happened to pick up a shift in my old department. I was the raker for that shift. I remembered the question she had asked me just a few days prior. I looked down into the liquid lava and sure enough, I could see myself. My reflection glared off the refined liquid material.

This reminded me of stories I've heard about when a silversmith is refining silver. I find it very interesting that a silversmith holds the silver in the middle of the fire where the flames are the hottest. The purpose for this is not to damage the silver being refined but, the silversmith knows the silver is durable enough to withstand the flames at the hottest point in order to burn away all of its impurities.

God knows that His creation is strong enough to withstand the flames of the refinery of life! He knows this because He promises to always be with us! He knows this because Jesus fought and already won every battle we will ever endure! He knows that we are mighty in Him! He knows that we are more than conquerors in Him! He knows the potential that lies within each of us!

Now, do we? Do we take Him at His Word? Do we believe what His

THE REFINERY

Word says? Do we believe that His ways are higher than ours? Do we believe that if He is for us who can be against us? Do we believe that our latter shall be greater than our former? Do we even believe we have a purpose? Do we believe that ALL things work together for our good – even the refining process?

The silversmith not only has to hold the silver in his hand the entire

GOD KNOWS THAT HIS CREATION IS STRONG ENOUGH TO WITHSTAND THE FLAMES OF THE REFINERY OF LIFE!

time it is on the flame, but he cannot take his eyes off of it for one second. If the silver is left even a moment too long in the fire it will be destroyed. The silversmith knows that the silver is fully refined when he can see his image in it. God watches over us at all times. Proverbs 15:3 says, "The eyes of the Lord are in every place, watching the evil and the good." Psalm 121:8 says, "The Lord will guard your going out and your coming in from this time forth and forever." He constantly keeps watch over us. Just because we go through some hard refining times in life doesn't mean He isn't there.

I think about this truth as I remember where I have come from and all that I have been through. Considering all I've been exposed to things could have still been worse. Its not because the enemy has spared me from any of his attacks or took it easy on me because of what I had been through already. It was God's mercy that spared me from many situations that could have been much worse! Before I ever received Jesus as my Lord and Savior, God was sparing me from even more pain. He was watching over my life before I ever gave my life to Him. He was watching over my life because of the purpose He placed in me when He created me.

No matter where we come from or how we are raised we will experience

NEVER ALONE

God-moments in our lives. Sometimes we are too young to understand the significance of these moments when they occur, but they still have a purpose. The purpose is to plants seeds in us to know there is more to this life than meets the eye.

I am reminded of Mama Rosa. Many times throughout my life I have thought back to this lady that I learned was my great-grandmother. After giving my heart to Christ, I knew she had planted seeds in me. I knew that God had not only heard her prayers, but honored them. He watched over me! He spared my life and now He has saved my soul!

> **HE WAS WATCHING OVER MY LIFE BEFORE I EVER GAVE MY LIFE TO HIM.**

There have been other God-moments that have intersected throughout my life before I gave my heart to Him. I remember the people who helped me when I was on the streets in L.A. I remember the teachers who reached out to me at school and pushed me to be more and to want more. I remember the people who would pick me up and take me to church. I would see things in them and in their life that I wanted. The things I saw in these people gave me hope that things could be different. My future didn't have to look like my past, but where I had come from would help me appreciate where I was going!

When God intersected my life with my wife's, things really changed. Neither of us were serving the Lord. Yet, He took her mess and broken pieces and my mess and broken pieces and put them together in a beautiful piece of artwork. If we could see the masterpiece in the spiritual realm, I know it would be on display in the finest of exhibits. We would stand and marvel at the beauty of the intricate details He has placed in our masterpiece of life. That is what He does with all of our lives! He takes broken, shattered pieces and puts them back together. The shards of brokenness from our lives

THE REFINERY

that cut us and will cut others too, He carefully mends and places into this beautiful work of art that is our lives. Only if we let Him. Only if we give Him access.

The refinery of life is no joke. It's hard and it can be discouraging. We must begin to understand that the refining process isn't meant to take us out, but to take us into what God has for us. We have to recognize that the refining process is meant to push us closer and closer to walking into our God-given destiny and purpose! As I said at the beginning of this chapter, we should never want God to quit refining us because as long as we live in this imperfect world, we need Him to keep pulling the impurities out of us! We need Him to keep making us more like Him. We want Him to see His reflection in us when He looks at us. Proverbs 27:19 says, "As water reflects the face, so one's life reflects the heart." Our heart is reflected in our actions. Does our life reflect Him?

Whether we are believers or not, we are not exempt from the refinery of life. To me, it makes no sense to go through *The Refinery* for nothing. It makes no sense to deal with all that life throws at us for nothing good to ever come out of it or us. We must understand that we have the ability to choose what comes out of our refining process. Are we helping God help us or not? Are we reflecting him? Can He see his reflection in our lives and our hearts? The Bible says in 1st Samuel that God doesn't look on our outward appearance or what we allow others to see. God looks on the heart of man. Proverbs 17:3 says, "Fire tests the purity of silver and gold, but the LORD tests the heart." As things develop and unfold in my life, both good and bad, I hope God can see more and more of Himself in me. I need His refining! My soul depends on it!

There is a powerful, victorious, fulfilling life through Christ. I did not say easy or without hardship or pain, but a life that can provide joy in the midst of trials. A life that can provide security in the midst of chaos. A life that can provide peace in the midst of stress. A life that provides hope for our future!

CHAPTER

15

PURPOSE FROM THE PAIN

"And they overcame him by the blood of the Lamb, and by the word of their testimony..."
Revelation 12:11 (KJV)

NEVER ALONE

There is a scripture that says God works all things out for our good. It goes on to say: "to them that love God, to them who are the called according to His purpose." You may be wondering, yeah, but do I even have a purpose? Of course you do! If you are here, which you are because you are reading this, you have a purpose! You can be sure that you have a purpose just because of the very fact that you exist! God does not create anything or anyone without a purpose!

Okay, now that we are all on the same page and know we have a purpose, how do we know if we are called by Him? John 1:12 says, "But as many as received Him, to them He gave the right to become children of God, even to those who believe in His name." To be called by God all we have to do is receive Jesus as our Lord and Savior. 2 Timothy 1:9 says, "He has saved us and called us to a holy life–not because of anything we have done but because of his own purpose and grace. This grace was given us in Christ Jesus before the beginning of time." We are called by Him for something great not because we have done anything great but, because Jesus has! He just loves His creation so much that He lets us become a part of His great plan.

Check out this next part: not only does He let us be a part of His great plan but 2 Corinthians 6:18 says, "'And, I will be a Father to you, and you will be my sons and daughters,' says the Lord Almighty." I don't know about you but between what I've been through and some of the things I've done this verse completely amazes me. Not only will He accept me and allow me to be used in His kingdom but He will also be my Father! He will look after me better than I am capable of looking after my own children. That's crazy right? I mean, I would do anything for my children. I would go to any lengths and do anything within my power to make sure they were cared for, provided for and protected. And He will do the same for me and for you!

I have never had a "normal" relationship with my earthly father. After all that I have experienced it is truly a miracle that I am the father I am today. It's

PURPOSE FROM THE PAIN

a miracle that I even wanted to be a father. God has taken every bad thing that has happened in my life big or small and turned it into good!

If you looked at me today, not knowing my story, you would never be able to tell where I have come from or what I have endured. You would never guess that this is my story. That is true for many of us. When we look at someone, we don't see the story that lies just below the surface. We can't tell, just by looking, the journey that each of us has been on. However, if we love God, His word says that ALL things will work out for our good! And not just for our good, but for the good of those lives that we affect or influence. Our lives are connected to other lives. That is the way God intended it to be. Everything we do, good or bad, affects those around us equally the same, good or bad.

For example, when a rock is thrown into water, the water around it is moved. The water is changed by the rock's influence – it creates a ripple. What kind of ripple effect are you having on those around you? What kind of ripple effect are those around you having on *you*?

I am reminded of my teachers in California who would always tell me, "Surround yourself with good people." I don't know why, but this advice always stuck with me. It made me really think, even in the hard times. If I wanted a good life and a good future, I needed good people in my life. I couldn't hang out with people who were breaking the law or I would end up breaking the law. I couldn't hang out with people who were doing drugs or I would do drugs. I couldn't hang out with people who were gang-banging or I would gang bang. It dawned on me that I may not have had control over what had happened to me in my childhood, but I did have control over who my friends were or were not.

Even though I didn't have control over what happened in my childhood, I do have control over the person I am today! I have control in choosing if I am going to be bitter or better from every obstacle I have had to face. I choose

NEVER ALONE

to be better! Not, just for myself, but for my wife and kids, my brother and sisters, my nieces and nephews and my friends and co-workers. My life affects them. And maybe, just maybe if one of them are going through a hard time, I can share what God has done in my own life. Then, they can see that by the grace of God, they can get through whatever it is they are going through!

The year 2015 was probably the hardest year yet for my family. That's a pretty bold statement considering all that I've experienced in my short 33 years. My family was hit with some pretty hard and serious things. Early on in the year it seemed to be one thing right after the other. We would no sooner get through one issue then another one would be right behind it. That's one of the reasons it was so difficult. We could hardly catch our breath between blows. Some things we knew were coming and we were able to somewhat prepare, but others hit us out of nowhere and left us to carry on the best we could. Sometimes it felt as though we weren't even making it from day to day, but from hour to hour.

One thing that we were able to somewhat prepare for was losing our home of 13 years. As a result of the immigration battle, we lost just about everything financially. Our house was the last thing to go. We knew it was coming so we were able to form an action plan to a certain degree. What happened next hit us out of nowhere and left no time to prepare.

My mother-in-law got sick and was admitted to the hospital. At first it didn't look too serious. There was a plan in place to get her up and going again, even talk of releasing her from the hospital to go home. Then things took a turn for the worse – worse than ever before.

About 1 or 2 a.m. on a Friday morning the hospital called my wife. They told Liz that her mom had given them permission to intubate her because she was having issues breathing. When Liz left the hospital late on Thursday night, she knew there were issues with her mom's breathing. The doctors were trying to get to the bottom of what was happening, but when Liz left,

PURPOSE FROM THE PAIN

her mom was still struggling to breath as she slept. So when the hospital said they were going to intubate her, Liz was relieved that her mom wouldn't have to struggle to breathe and could finally get some rest.

"She's been in there almost a week and hasn't been able to rest. Maybe now at least her body can get some relief while the doctors figure out what to do next," she said. We decided to get up and go to the hospital. Liz wanted to be with her mom. We left the kids home with Nate so they could sleep. I would go back home to get them off to school.

The door was open as we walked up to my mother-in-law's room, but a nurse stopped us from going in. "Please wait outside," she said as she closed the door. They were in the process of putting the tube in. It seemed like we waited in that hall forever. Finally they told us to go to the waiting room. They said they would come and get us when we were allowed to go back to the room.

"She'll be okay," Liz said. "I watched my dad come off a vent and she will too. She just needs to rest while they figure out what to do next."

What happened over the next few weeks and months ripped my wife apart. The following morning a special team was called in to transport my mother-in-law via Lifeline to one of the major hospitals in downtown Indianapolis. For the next 11 days either Liz, her dad, her brother or her sister were camped out at the hospital. Someone stayed with my mother-in-law at all times. I watched my wife as she juggled life. She kept watch and stayed informed with all of her mother's medical situations while staying connected to our five kids at home. Not only was this happening with my mother-in-law, it was also nearing the end of the school year and Nate's high school graduation and party was coming up.

Four days before Nate graduated my mother-in-law passed away. Nothing could have prepared us for that. I loved my mother-in-law. She was always so good to me. My wife and kids loved her and were very close to her. My heart

NEVER ALONE

broke because she was gone. My heart broke because my wife and kids were hurting and there was nothing I could do it make it any better for them. My heart broke because I lost a part of my wife that day. Liz went through a very dark and difficult time. Sometimes, I felt helpless because I just wanted my wife back. I didn't know how to deal with her grief.

Right after Nate's graduation ceremony we had to head to Virginia for my mother-in-law's funeral. Within seven days we had lost Liz's mom, Nate graduated and we had the funeral. Two, once-in-a-lifetime events – one brought immense joy and pride and the other brought overwhelming grief and pain – all within a week of each other. I look back now and wonder how we made it through those days. I have only one answer: God!

About six-weeks after the funeral we had to move from our home. In a span of seven weeks my wife lost her mother and our family home of 13 years. I watched her slip into hopelessness, grief, anger and despair. All I could do was pray that God would heal her broken heart. That He would bring her back to us, back to me! I needed her back! He did bring her back. It took some time but, He did it. She's not the same. I'll never have her back like she was before she lost her mother, but she has allowed the Lord to help her deal with her grief and there are some beautiful strengths that have surfaced through it all. God has and still is making something beautiful out of her pain.

That is what He does. He doesn't leave us like He found us. It doesn't matter where we start. It only matters where we finish. Like I said in the first chapter, we don't get a say in the starting point of our life, but we ALWAYS get a say in where we finish. We choose how we act. We choose how we interact with others. We choose if we let the enemy of our souls influence and direct our lives. We choose if we serve the God who created us. We choose if we accept Jesus Christ as our Lord and Savior. We choose! We choose not to let those things that have happened to us control us and our future. We choose not to believe the lies of the enemy. We choose not to feel sorry for ourselves. We choose to let God take our mess and turn it into something

PURPOSE FROM THE PAIN

awesome. We choose to keep going, to keep fighting, to keep believing for what God has for us. We choose if purpose comes out of our pain!

Even when I was young and I realized all of the horrible things that were happening, in my heart I knew there had to be more. I needed to believe there was more for me in life than poverty, abandonment, abuse, rejection – and I wanted it! Even before I accepted Jesus into my life, I knew there had to be more to this life. There had to be something greater.

I don't want anyone to walk away from my story feeling sorry for me! Why should you? I don't feel sorry for me! Everyone goes through hard things. Everyone has a story. Despite what I have been through, I have so much to thank God for. God's grace, mercy, protection and love over my life continually overwhelm me! He has been so good to me! He put breath in my body and made my legs to walk. Even when I didn't know Him He provided for me and protected me on the streets of L. A. Not only that, but He got me off of those streets.

I have watched Him heal and restore broken relationships. I have watched Him spare my life. I have felt Him change and soften my heart. I have watched Him give me favor with judges. I have watched Him make a way out of no way! I have watched Him give me jobs making enough money to support my family despite my lack of education. He has helped me pass classes, go through training and get certifications even though I never learned how to read or write English properly.

I have watched Him give me the wife and children I always wanted – a family that is there for each other and takes care of each other. I have watched my children being born and every time I marveled at God and His creation. How can anyone question if there is a God? I have watched Him heal my son and my wife. I have watched Him provide for my family with only one income.

I have felt Him give me strength when I wasn't sure if I could keep going.

NEVER ALONE

I have watched Him put things back together in my life that looked broken beyond repair. I have watched Him give my sister and her husband a baby after struggling with infertility for five years and then He went ahead and gave them another one. I felt the comfort and peace He brought to my wife and I through the loss of our baby. I have watched Him walk through grief and despair with my wife, being for her what I couldn't be and helping her grow through that process. He helped me raise three kids and continues to help me raise four more. He is more than good to me! "And my tongue shall talk of your righteousness and praise all the day long," Psalm 35:28.

> "FOR I AM CONVINCED THAT NEITHER DEATH NOR LIFE, NEITHER ANGELS NOR DEMONS, NEITHER THE PRESENT NOR THE FUTURE, NOR ANY POWERS, NEITHER HEIGHT NOR DEPTH, NOR ANYTHING ELSE IN ALL CREATION, WILL BE ABLE TO SEPARATE US FROM THE LOVE OF GOD THAT IS IN CHRIST JESUS OUR LORD."
> ROMANS 8:38-39.

You see, everything good and bad that has happened in my life points me to this: NOTHING can separate us from the love of God! Nothing we have had control over – nothing we haven't had control over. Nothing we have done – nothing that has been done to us can make God love us any less than He did when He created us! That is real love! My whole world changed when I realized God loved me like this!

Psalm 78:4 says, "We will not hide them from our children but, we will tell to the generation to come the praise worthy deeds of the Lord and His might

PURPOSE FROM THE PAIN

and the wonderful works that He has performed." My story, your story – our testimony – is so important. Not only are we overcomers by the blood of the Lamb and word of our testimony, but we have to let others know what God has done for us! What He has delivered us from! We have to tell our children and our children's children. We have to tell anyone who will listen what the almighty, powerful God has done and continues to do for His creation. We must do this so, "That the generation to come might know them, that the children still to be born might arise and recount them to their children. That they might set their hope in God and not forget the works of God, but might keep His commandments," Psalm 78:6-7. A lot of people are searching for love, searching for answers, they are searching for hope. We have that answer! Jesus!

I have overcome many things in my life – abandonment, rejection, anger, pride, abuse, insecurity, poverty, homelessness, cultural barriers, racial barriers, educational barriers and language barriers, even death. A few of these things I am still overcoming. Some people get upset and frustrated with God because life can be hard. There can be so much in life to go through and to overcome. It is sad that people completely overlook this truth: not only does God want you to overcome, but He created you to overcome! Romans 8:37 says, "No, in all these things we are more than conquerors through Him who loved us." 1 John 4:4 says, "You, dear children, are from God and have overcome them, because the one who is in you is greater than the one who is in the world."

If I could sit down with you right now, this very second as you are reading this book, I would ask you to pause for a moment. I would look you in the eye and tell you that God does exist and Jesus is His son. I would tell you that He loves you! No matter where you've come from or what you've done, He loves you! I would tell you that He desires to have a relationship with you. I would look you in the eye and tell you He is the answer! To every problem and every question, He is the answer! I would tell you, without a doubt, that you are

NEVER ALONE

Never Alone! God is always intersecting moments into our lives that point to Him, letting us know He is there and He wants us to call on Him.

Looking back over my life, even reading this book – my story that I sometimes can't believe is mine – I see that I was *Never Alone*! He was always there! I may not know your story, but I know you have one. I also know that God created you for a purpose and that there is great *Purpose Through the Pain*! Now that you know, what will you do? It's up to you!

AFTERWORD

Thank you for taking this journey and letting me share my life with you. I have shared many things with you. Some of these things were hard to put out there but, I felt I had no choice. If I had not shown you exactly what I have came through, you would not have an accurate picture of where God has brought me from! Of course there are details left out because some are better left unsaid, but I needed you to know – to understand what ALL God has done! Because if He did it for me He WILL do it for you! To God be ALL the glory!

God has healed and continues to heal my heart in different areas. I am thankful that He continues to mend the relationship between me and my mother. I am thankful that my children can know and have memories with their "Abuela".

It is my prayer that all of my family experiences Jesus in a real, tangible way, like I have. When it's too late to change what's happened in the past, He can change me! He can help me to not to continue the cycle! He makes everything right!

Juan Canales
June 2017

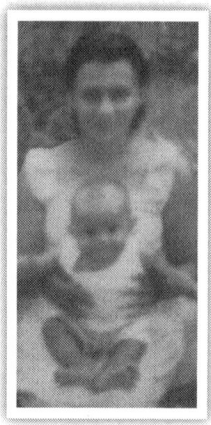
The only baby picture I have – my mom and me in Honduras.

Our apartment in South Central L.A. above the market.

Johana, Cristian and I when we lived on Arapahoe.

My first school picture in the U.S. This was shortly before my parents went back to Honduras.

My mom, Johana, Cristian and I at the San Pedro Fish Market.

Me around age 14 on Marguerite Street when I drove the car backwards down the street.

Liz and me when we were dating in Indianapolis.

Liz, Nate and me on our wedding day February 2, 2002.

Our second Christmas as a Family of Five.

Taking care of Alex during his battle with laryngomalacia.

Johana's graduation day!

Christian's graduation day!

Johana's wedding day!

Cristian's wedding day!

Surrounded by family and friends the day I was awarded Permanent Residency in Chicago, IL.

Citizenship day!

Nate's graduation with Papaw and Grandma.

One big, happy family!

Made in the USA
Lexington, KY
26 June 2017